JAPANESE
V O C A B U L A R Y

FOR ENGLISH SPEAKERS

ENGLISH-JAPANESE

The most useful words
To expand your lexicon and sharpen
your language skills

3000 words

Japanese vocabulary for English speakers - 3000 words

By Andrey Taranov

T&P Books vocabularies are intended for helping you learn, memorize and review foreign words. The dictionary is divided into themes, covering all major spheres of everyday activities, business, science, culture, etc.

The process of learning words using T&P Books' theme-based dictionaries gives you the following advantages:

- Correctly grouped source information predetermines success at subsequent stages of word memorization
- Availability of words derived from the same root allowing memorization of word units (rather than separate words)
- Small units of words facilitate the process of establishing associative links needed for consolidation of vocabulary
- Level of language knowledge can be estimated by the number of learned words

T&P Books Publishing
www.tpbooks.com

ISBN: 978-1-78314-246-0

This book is also available in E-book formats.
Please visit www.tpbooks.com or the major online bookstores.

JAPANESE VOCABULARY
for English speakers

T&P Books vocabularies are intended to help you learn, memorize, and review foreign words. The vocabulary contains over 3000 commonly used words arranged thematically.

- Vocabulary contains the most commonly used words
- Recommended as an addition to any language course
- Meets the needs of beginners and advanced learners of foreign languages
- Convenient for daily use, revision sessions, and self-testing activities
- Allows you to assess your vocabulary

Special features of the vocabulary

- Words are organized according to their meaning, not alphabetically
- Words are presented in three columns to facilitate the reviewing and self-testing processes
- Words in groups are divided into small blocks to facilitate the learning process
- The vocabulary offers a convenient and simple transcription of each foreign word

The vocabulary has 101 topics including:

Basic Concepts, Numbers, Colors, Months, Seasons, Units of Measurement, Clothing & Accessories, Food & Nutrition, Restaurant, Family Members, Relatives, Character, Feelings, Emotions, Diseases, City, Town, Sightseeing, Shopping, Money, House, Home, Office, Working in the Office, Import & Export, Marketing, Job Search, Sports, Education, Computer, Internet, Tools, Nature, Countries, Nationalities and more …

T&P BOOKS' THEME-BASED DICTIONARIES

The Correct System for Memorizing Foreign Words

Acquiring vocabulary is one of the most important elements of learning a foreign language, because words allow us to express our thoughts, ask questions, and provide answers. An inadequate vocabulary can impede communication with a foreigner and make it difficult to understand a book or movie well.

The pace of activity in all spheres of modern life, including the learning of modern languages, has increased. Today, we need to memorize large amounts of information (grammar rules, foreign words, etc.) within a short period. However, this does not need to be difficult. All you need to do is to choose the right training materials, learn a few special techniques, and develop your individual training system.

Having a system is critical to the process of language learning. Many people fail to succeed in this regard; they cannot master a foreign language because they fail to follow a system comprised of selecting materials, organizing lessons, arranging new words to be learned, and so on. The lack of a system causes confusion and eventually, lowers self-confidence.

T&P Books' theme-based dictionaries can be included in the list of elements needed for creating an effective system for learning foreign words. These dictionaries were specially developed for learning purposes and are meant to help students effectively memorize words and expand their vocabulary.

Generally speaking, the process of learning words consists of three main elements:

- Reception (creation or acquisition) of a training material, such as a word list
- Work aimed at memorizing new words
- Work aimed at reviewing the learned words, such as self-testing

All three elements are equally important since they determine the quality of work and the final result. All three processes require certain skills and a well-thought-out approach.

New words are often encountered quite randomly when learning a foreign language and it may be difficult to include them all in a unified list. As a result, these words remain written on scraps of paper, in book margins, textbooks, and so on. In order to systematize such words, we have to create and continually update a "book of new words." A paper notebook, a netbook, or a tablet PC can be used for these purposes.

This "book of new words" will be your personal, unique list of words. However, it will only contain the words that you came across during the learning process. For example, you might have written down the words "Sunday," "Tuesday," and "Friday." However, there are additional words for days of the week, for example, "Saturday," that are missing, and your list of words would be incomplete. Using a theme dictionary, in addition to the "book of new words," is a reasonable solution to this problem.

The theme-based dictionary may serve as the basis for expanding your vocabulary.

It will be your big "book of new words" containing the most frequently used words of a foreign language already included. There are quite a few theme-based dictionaries available, and you should ensure that you make the right choice in order to get the maximum benefit from your purchase.

Therefore, we suggest using theme-based dictionaries from T&P Books Publishing as an aid to learning foreign words. Our books are specially developed for effective use in the sphere of vocabulary systematization, expansion and review.

Theme-based dictionaries are not a magical solution to learning new words. However, they can serve as your main database to aid foreign-language acquisition. Apart from theme dictionaries, you can have copybooks for writing down new words, flash cards, glossaries for various texts, as well as other resources; however, a good theme dictionary will always remain your primary collection of words.

T&P Books' theme-based dictionaries are specialty books that contain the most frequently used words in a language.

The main characteristic of such dictionaries is the division of words into themes. For example, the *City* theme contains the words "street," "crossroads," "square," "fountain," and so on. The *Talking* theme might contain words like "to talk," "to ask," "question," and "answer".

All the words in a theme are divided into smaller units, each comprising 3–5 words. Such an arrangement improves the perception of words and makes the learning process less tiresome. Each unit contains a selection of words with similar meanings or identical roots. This allows you to learn words in small groups and establish other associative links that have a positive effect on memorization.

The words on each page are placed in three columns: a word in your native language, its translation, and its transcription. Such positioning allows for the use of techniques for effective memorization. After closing the translation column, you can flip through and review foreign words, and vice versa. "This is an easy and convenient method of review – one that we recommend you do often."

Our theme-based dictionaries contain transcriptions for all the foreign words. Unfortunately, none of the existing transcriptions are able to convey the exact nuances of foreign pronunciation. That is why we recommend using the transcriptions only as a supplementary learning aid. Correct pronunciation can only be acquired with the help of sound. Therefore our collection includes audio theme-based dictionaries.

The process of learning words using T&P Books' theme-based dictionaries gives you the following advantages:

- You have correctly grouped source information, which predetermines your success at subsequent stages of word memorization
- Availability of words derived from the same root (lazy, lazily, lazybones), allowing you to memorize word units instead of separate words
- Small units of words facilitate the process of establishing associative links needed for consolidation of vocabulary
- You can estimate the number of learned words and hence your level of language knowledge
- The dictionary allows for the creation of an effective and high-quality revision process
- You can revise certain themes several times, modifying the revision methods and techniques
- Audio versions of the dictionaries help you to work out the pronunciation of words and develop your skills of auditory word perception

The T&P Books' theme-based dictionaries are offered in several variants differing in the number of words: 1.500, 3.000, 5.000, 7.000, and 9.000 words. There are also dictionaries containing 15,000 words for some language combinations. Your choice of dictionary will depend on your knowledge level and goals.

We sincerely believe that our dictionaries will become your trusty assistant in learning foreign languages and will allow you to easily acquire the necessary vocabulary.

TABLE OF CONTENTS

PRONUNCIATION GUIDE

Hiragana	Katakana	Rōmaji	Japanese example	T&P phonetic alphabet	English example

Consonants

Hiragana	Katakana	Rōmaji	Japanese example	T&P phonetic alphabet	English example
あ	ア	a	あなた	[a]	shorter than in ask
い	イ	i	いす	[i], [i:]	feet, Peter
う	ウ	u	うた	[u], [u:]	book, shoe
え	エ	e	いいえ	[e]	elm, medal
お	オ	o	しお	[ɔ]	bottle, doctor
や	ヤ	ya	やすみ	[ja]	young, yard
ゆ	ユ	yu	ふゆ	[ju]	youth, usually
よ	ヨ	yo	ようす	[jɔ]	New York

Syllables

Hiragana	Katakana	Rōmaji	Japanese example	T&P phonetic alphabet	English example
ば	バ	b	ばん	[b]	baby, book
ち	チ	ch	ちち	[tʃ]	cheese
だ	ダ	d	からだ	[d]	day, doctor
ふ	フ	f	ひふ	[f]	face, food
が	ガ	g	がっこう	[g]	game, gold
は	ハ	h	はは	[h]	home, have
じ	ジ	j	じしょ	[dʒ]	joke, general
か	カ	k	かぎ	[k]	clock, kiss
む	ム	m	さむらい	[m]	magic, milk
に	ニ	n	にもつ	[n]	name, normal
ぱ	パ	p	パン	[p]	pencil, private
ら	ラ	r	いくら	[r]	rice, radio
さ	サ	s	あさ	[s]	city, boss
し	シ	sh	わたし	[ɕ]	sheep, shop
た	タ	t	ふた	[t]	tourist, trip
つ	ツ	ts	いくつ	[ts]	cats, tsetse fly
わ	ワ	w	わた	[w]	vase, winter
ざ	ザ	z	ざっし	[dz]	beads, kids

ABBREVIATIONS
used in the vocabulary

ab.	-	about
adj	-	adjective
adv	-	adverb
anim.	-	animate
as adj	-	attributive noun used as adjective
e.g.	-	for example
etc.	-	et cetera
fam.	-	familiar
fem.	-	feminine
form.	-	formal
inanim.	-	inanimate
masc.	-	masculine
math	-	mathematics
mil.	-	military
n	-	noun
pl	-	plural
pron.	-	pronoun
sb	-	somebody
sing.	-	singular
sth	-	something
v aux	-	auxiliary verb
vi	-	intransitive verb
vi, vt	-	intransitive, transitive verb
vt	-	transitive verb

BASIC CONCEPTS

1. Pronouns

I, me	私	watashi
you	あなた	anata
he	彼	kare
she	彼女	kanojo
we	私たち	watashi tachi
you (to a group)	あなたがた	anata ga ta
they	彼らは	karera wa

2. Greetings. Salutations

Hello! (fam.)	やあ！	yā!
Hello! (form.)	こんにちは！	konnichiwa!
Good morning!	おはよう！	ohayō!
Good afternoon!	こんにちは！	konnichiwa!
Good evening!	こんばんは！	konbanwa!
to say hello	こんにちはと言う	konnichiwa to iu
Hi! (hello)	やあ！	yā!
greeting (n)	挨拶	aisatsu
to greet (vt)	挨拶する	aisatsu suru
How are you?	元気？	genki ?
How are you? (form.)	お元気ですか？	wo genki desu ka?
How are you? (fam.)	元気？	genki ?
What's new?	調子はどう？	chōshi ha dō ?
Bye-Bye! Goodbye!	さようなら！	sayōnara!
Goodbye! (form.)	さようなら！	sayōnara!
Bye! (fam.)	バイバイ！	baibai!
See you soon!	じゃあね！	jā ne!
Farewell!	さらば！	saraba !
to say goodbye	別れを告げる	wakare wo tsugeru
So long!	またね！	mata ne!
Thank you!	ありがとう！	arigatō!
Thank you very much!	どうもありがとう！	dōmo arigatō!
You're welcome	どういたしまして	dōitashimashite
Don't mention it!	礼なんていいよ	rei nante ī yo
It was nothing	どういたしまして	dōitashimashite

Excuse me! (fam.)	失礼！	shitsurei!
Excuse me! (form.)	失礼致します！	shitsurei itashi masu!
to excuse (forgive)	許す	yurusu

to apologize (vi)	謝る	ayamaru
My apologies	おわび致します！	owabi itashi masu!
I'm sorry!	ごめんなさい！	gomennasai!
to forgive (vt)	許す	yurusu
It's okay!	大丈夫です！	daijōbu desu!
please (adv)	お願い	onegai

Don't forget!	忘れないで！	wasure nai de!
Certainly!	もちろん！	mochiron!
Of course not!	そんなことないよ！	sonna koto nai yo!
Okay! (I agree)	オーケー！	ōkē!
That's enough!	もう十分だ！	mō jūbun da!

3. Questions

Who?	誰？	dare ?
What?	何？	nani ?
Where? (at, in)	どこに？	doko ni ?
Where (to)?	どちらへ？	dochira he ?
From where?	どこから？	doko kara ?
When?	いつ？	itsu ?
Why? (What for?)	なんで？	nande ?
Why? (reason)	どうして？	dōshite ?

What for?	何のために？	nan no tame ni ?
How? (in what way)	どうやって？	dō yatte?
What? (What kind of ...?)	どんな ？	donna?
Which?	どちらの…？	dochira no … ?

To whom?	誰に？	dare ni ?
About whom?	誰のこと？	dare no koto ?
About what?	何のこと？	nannokoto ?
With whom?	誰と？	dare to ?

How many?	いくつ？	ikutsu ?
How much?	いくら？	ikura ?
Whose?	誰のもの？	Dare no mono ?

4. Prepositions

with (accompanied by)	…と、…と共に	… to, totomoni
without	…なしで	… nashi de
to (indicating direction)	…へ	… he
about (talking ~ ...)	…について	… ni tsuite

| before (in time) | …の前に | … no mae ni |
| in front of … | …の正面に | … no shōmen ni |

under (beneath, below)	下に	shita ni
above (over)	上側に	uwagawa ni
on (atop)	上に	ue ni
from (off, out of)	…から	… kara
of (made from)	…製の	… sei no

| in (e.g., ~ ten minutes) | …で | … de |
| over (across the top of) | …を越えて | … wo koe te |

5. Function words. Adverbs. Part 1

Where? (at, in)	どこに？	doko ni ?
here (adv)	ここで	kokode
there (adv)	そこで	sokode

| somewhere (to be) | どこかで | doko ka de |
| nowhere (not anywhere) | どこにも | doko ni mo |

| by (near, beside) | 近くで | chikaku de |
| by the window | 窓辺に | mado beni |

Where (to)?	どちらへ？	dochira he ?
here (e.g., come ~!)	こちらへ	kochira he
there (e.g., to go ~)	そこへ	soko he
from here (adv)	ここから	koko kara
from there (adv)	そこから	soko kara

| close (adv) | そばに | soba ni |
| far (adv) | 遠くに | tōku ni |

near (e.g., ~ Paris)	近く	chikaku
nearby (adv)	近くに	chikaku ni
not far (adv)	遠くない	tōku nai

left (adj)	左の	hidari no
on the left	左に	hidari ni
to the left	左へ	hidari he

right (adj)	右の	migi no
on the right	右に	migi ni
to the right	右へ	migi he

in front (adv)	前に	mae ni
front (as adj)	前の	mae no
ahead (look ~)	前方へ	zenpō he
behind (adv)	後ろに	ushiro ni
from behind	後ろから	ushiro kara

back (towards the rear)	後ろへ	ushiro he
middle	中央	chūō
in the middle	中央に	chūō ni
at the side	側面から	sokumen kara
everywhere (adv)	どこでも	doko demo
around (in all directions)	…の周りを	… no mawari wo
from inside	中から	naka kara
somewhere (to go)	どこかへ	dokoka he
straight (directly)	真っ直ぐに	massugu ni
back (e.g., come ~)	戻って	modotte
from anywhere	どこからでも	doko kara demo
from somewhere	どこからか	doko kara ka
firstly (adv)	第一に	dai ichi ni
secondly (adv)	第二に	dai ni ni
thirdly (adv)	第三に	dai san ni
suddenly (adv)	急に	kyū ni
at first (adv)	初めは	hajime wa
for the first time	初めて	hajimete
long before …	…かなり前に	…kanari mae ni
anew (over again)	新たに	arata ni
for good (adv)	永遠に	eien ni
never (adv)	一度も	ichi do mo
again (adv)	再び	futatabi
now (adv)	今	ima
often (adv)	よく	yoku
then (adv)	あのとき	ano toki
urgently (quickly)	至急に	shikyū ni
usually (adv)	普通は	futsū wa
by the way, …	ところで、…	tokorode, …
possible (that is ~)	可能な	kanō na
probably (adv)	恐らく［おそらく］	osoraku
maybe (adv)	ことによると	kotoni yoru to
besides …	それに	soreni
that's why …	従って	shitagatte
in spite of …	…にもかかわらず	… ni mo kakawara zu
thanks to …	…のおかげで	… no okage de
what (pron.)	何	nani
that (conj.)	…ということ	… toyuu koto
something	何か	nani ka
anything (something)	何か	nani ka
nothing	何もない	nani mo nai
who (pron.)	誰	dare
someone	ある人	aru hito

somebody	誰か	dare ka
nobody	誰も…ない	dare mo … nai
nowhere (a voyage to ~)	どこへも	doko he mo
nobody's	誰の…でもない	dare no … de mo nai
somebody's	誰かの	dare ka no
so (I'm ~ glad)	とても	totemo
also (as well)	また	mata
too (as well)	も	mo

6. Function words. Adverbs. Part 2

Why?	どうして？	dōshite ?
for some reason	なぜか [何故か]	naze ka
because …	なぜなら	nazenara
for some purpose	何らかの理由で	nanrakano riyū de
and	と	to
or	または	matawa
but	でも	demo
for (e.g., ~ me)	…のために	… no tame ni
too (~ many people)	…すぎる	… sugiru
only (exclusively)	もっぱら	moppara
exactly (adv)	正確に	seikaku ni
about (more or less)	約	yaku
approximately (adv)	おおよそ	ōyoso
approximate (adj)	おおよその	ōyosono
almost (adv)	ほとんど	hotondo
the rest	残り	nokori
the other (second)	もう一方の	mōippōno
other (different)	他の	hokano
each (adj)	各	kaku
any (no matter which)	どれでも	dore demo
many (adv)	多くの	ōku no
much (adv)	多量の	taryō no
many people	多くの人々	ōku no hitobito
all (everyone)	あらゆる人	arayuru hito
in return for …	…の返礼として	… no henrei toshite
in exchange (adv)	引き換えに	hikikae ni
by hand (made)	手で	te de
hardly (negative opinion)	ほとんど…ない	hotondo … nai
probably (adv)	恐らく [おそらく]	osoraku
on purpose (adv)	わざと	wazato
by accident (adv)	偶然に	gūzen ni
very (adv)	非常に	hijō ni

for example (adv)	例えば	tatoeba
between	間	kan
among	…の間で	… no made
so much (such a lot)	たくさん	takusan
especially (adv)	特に	tokuni

NUMBERS. MISCELLANEOUS

7. Cardinal numbers. Part 1

0 zero	ゼロ	zero
1 one	一	ichi
2 two	二	ni
3 three	三	san
4 four	四	yon
5 five	五	go
6 six	六	roku
7 seven	七	nana
8 eight	八	hachi
9 nine	九	kyū
10 ten	十	jū
11 eleven	十一	jū ichi
12 twelve	十二	jū ni
13 thirteen	十三	jū san
14 fourteen	十四	jū yon
15 fifteen	十五	jū go
16 sixteen	十六	jū roku
17 seventeen	十七	jū shichi
18 eighteen	十八	jū hachi
19 nineteen	十九	jū kyū
20 twenty	二十	ni jū
21 twenty-one	二十一	ni jū ichi
22 twenty-two	二十二	ni jū ni
23 twenty-three	二十三	ni jū san
30 thirty	三十	san jū
31 thirty-one	三一	san jū ichi
32 thirty-two	三二	san jū ni
33 thirty-three	三三	san jū san
40 forty	四十	yon jū
41 forty-one	四一	yon jū ichi
42 forty-two	四二	yon jū ni
43 forty-three	四三	yon jū san
50 fifty	五十	go jū
51 fifty-one	五十一	go jū ichi
52 fifty-two	五十二	go jū ni

53 fifty-three	五十三	go jū san
60 sixty	六十	roku jū
61 sixty-one	六十一	roku jū ichi
62 sixty-two	六十二	roku jū ni
63 sixty-three	六十三	roku jū san
70 seventy	七十	nana jū
71 seventy-one	七十一	nana jū ichi
72 seventy-two	七十二	nana jū ni
73 seventy-three	七十三	nana jū san
80 eighty	八十	hachi jū
81 eighty-one	八十一	hachi jū ichi
82 eighty-two	八十二	hachi jū ni
83 eighty-three	八十三	hachi jū san
90 ninety	九十	kyū jū
91 ninety-one	九十一	kyū jū ichi
92 ninety-two	九十二	kyū jū ni
93 ninety-three	九十三	kyū jū san

8. Cardinal numbers. Part 2

100 one hundred	百	hyaku
200 two hundred	二百	ni hyaku
300 three hundred	三百	san byaku
400 four hundred	四百	yon hyaku
500 five hundred	五百	go hyaku
600 six hundred	六百	roppyaku
700 seven hundred	七百	nana hyaku
800 eight hundred	八百	happyaku
900 nine hundred	九百	kyū hyaku
1000 one thousand	千	sen
2000 two thousand	二千	nisen
3000 three thousand	三千	sanzen
10000 ten thousand	一万	ichiman
one hundred thousand	10万	jyūman
million	百万	hyakuman
billion	十億	jūoku

9. Ordinal numbers

first (adj)	第一の	dai ichi no
second (adj)	第二の	dai ni no
third (adj)	第三の	dai san no
fourth (adj)	第四の	dai yon no

fifth (adj)	第五の	dai go no
sixth (adj)	第六の	dai roku no
seventh (adj)	第七の	dai nana no
eighth (adj)	第八の	dai hachi no
ninth (adj)	第九の	dai kyū no
tenth (adj)	第十の	dai jū no

COLOURS. UNITS OF MEASUREMENT

10. Colors

color	色	iro
shade (tint)	色合い	iroai
hue	色相	shikisō
rainbow	虹	niji
white (adj)	白い	shiroi
black (adj)	黒い	kuroi
gray (adj)	灰色の	haīro no
green (adj)	緑の	midori no
yellow (adj)	黄色い	kīroi
red (adj)	赤い	akai
blue (adj)	青い	aoi
light blue (adj)	水色の	mizu iro no
pink (adj)	ピンクの	pinku no
orange (adj)	オレンジの	orenji no
violet (adj)	紫色の	murasaki iro no
brown (adj)	茶色の	chairo no
golden (adj)	金色の	kiniro no
silvery (adj)	銀色の	giniro no
beige (adj)	ベージュの	bēju no
cream (adj)	クリームの	kurīmu no
turquoise (adj)	ターコイズブルーの	tākoizuburū no
cherry red (adj)	チェリーレッドの	cherī reddo no
lilac (adj)	ライラックの	rairakku no
crimson (adj)	クリムゾンの	kurimuzon no
light (adj)	薄い	usui
dark (adj)	濃い	koi
bright, vivid (adj)	鮮やかな	azayaka na
colored (pencils)	色の	iro no
color (e.g., ~ film)	カラー…	karā…
black-and-white (adj)	白黒の	shirokuro no
plain (one-colored)	単色の	tanshoku no
multicolored (adj)	色とりどりの	irotoridori no

11. Units of measurement

weight	重さ	omo sa
length	長さ	naga sa
width	幅	haba
height	高さ	taka sa
depth	深さ	fuka sa
volume	体積	taiseki
area	面積	menseki

gram	グラム	guramu
milligram	ミリグラム	miriguramu
kilogram	キログラム	kiroguramu
ton	トン	ton
pound	ポンド	pondo
ounce	オンス	onsu

meter	メートル	mētoru
millimeter	ミリメートル	mirimētoru
centimeter	センチメートル	senchimētoru
kilometer	キロメートル	kiromētoru
mile	マイル	mairu

inch	インチ	inchi
foot	フィート	fīto
yard	ヤード	yādo

| square meter | 平方メートル | heihō mētoru |
| hectare | ヘクタール | hekutāru |

liter	リットル	rittoru
degree	度	do
volt	ボルト	boruto
ampere	アンペア	anpea
horsepower	馬力	bariki

quantity	数量	sūryō
a little bit of ...	少し	sukoshi
half	半分	hanbun

| dozen | ダース | dāsu |
| piece (item) | 一個 | ikko |

| size | 大きさ | ōki sa |
| scale (map ~) | 縮尺 | shukushaku |

minimal (adj)	極小の	kyokushō no
the smallest (adj)	最小の	saishō no
medium (adj)	中位の	chūi no
maximal (adj)	極大の	kyokudai no
the largest (adj)	最大の	saidai no

12. Containers

jar (glass)	ジャー、瓶	jā, bin
can	缶	kan
bucket	バケツ	baketsu
barrel	樽	taru
basin (for washing)	たらい [盥]	tarai
tank (for liquid, gas)	タンク	tanku
hip flask	スキットル	sukittoru
jerrycan	ジェリカン	jerikan
cistern (tank)	積荷タンク	tsumini tanku
mug	マグカップ	magukappu
cup (of coffee, etc.)	カップ	kappu
saucer	ソーサー	sōsā
glass (tumbler)	ガラスのコップ	garasu no koppu
wineglass	ワイングラス	wain gurasu
saucepan	両手鍋	ryō tenabe
bottle (~ of wine)	ボトル	botoru
neck (of the bottle)	ネック	nekku
carafe	デキャンター	dekyanta
pitcher (earthenware)	水差し	mizusashi
vessel (container)	器	utsuwa
pot (crock)	鉢	hachi
vase	花瓶	kabin
bottle (~ of perfume)	瓶	bin
vial, small bottle	バイアル	bai aru
tube (of toothpaste)	チューブ	chūbu
sack (bag)	南京袋	nankinbukuro
bag (paper ~, plastic ~)	袋	fukuro
pack (of cigarettes, etc.)	箱	hako
box (e.g., shoebox)	箱	hako
crate	木箱	ki bako
basket	かご [籠]	kago

MAIN VERBS

13. The most important verbs. Part 1

to advise (vt)	助言する	jogen suru
to agree (say yes)	同意する	dōi suru
to answer (vi, vt)	回答する	kaitō suru
to apologize (vi)	謝る	ayamaru
to arrive (vi)	到着する	tōchaku suru
to ask (~ oneself)	問う	tō
to ask (~ sb to do sth)	頼む	tanomu
to be (vi)	ある	aru
to be afraid	怖がる	kowagaru
to be hungry	腹をすかす	hara wo sukasu
to be interested in ...	…に興味がある	… ni kyōmi ga aru
to be needed	必要である	hitsuyō de aru
to be surprised	驚く	odoroku
to be thirsty	喉が渇く	nodo ga kawaku
to begin (vt)	始める	hajimeru
to belong to ...	所有物である	shoyū butsu de aru
to boast (vi)	自慢する	jiman suru
to break (split into pieces)	折る、壊す	oru, kowasu
to call (for help)	求める	motomeru
can (v aux)	できる	dekiru
to catch (vt)	捕らえる	toraeru
to change (vt)	変える	kaeru
to choose (select)	選択する	sentaku suru
to come down	下りる	oriru
to come in (enter)	入る	hairu
to compare (vt)	比較する	hikaku suru
to complain (vi, vt)	不平を言う	fuhei wo iu
to confuse (mix up)	混同する	kondō suru
to continue (vt)	続ける	tsuzukeru
to control (vt)	管制する	kansei suru
to cook (dinner)	料理をする	ryōri wo suru
to cost (vt)	かかる	kakaru
to count (add up)	計算する	keisan suru
to count on ...	…を頼りにする	… wo tayori ni suru
to create (vt)	創造する	sōzō suru
to cry (weep)	泣く	naku

14. The most important verbs. Part 2

to deceive (vi, vt)	だます	damasu
to decorate (tree, street)	飾る	kazaru
to defend (a country, etc.)	防衛する	bōei suru
to demand (request firmly)	要求する	yōkyū suru
to dig (vt)	掘る	horu
to discuss (vt)	討議する	tōgi suru
to do (vt)	する	suru
to doubt (have doubts)	疑う	utagau
to drop (let fall)	落とす	otosu
to excuse (forgive)	許す	yurusu
to exist (vi)	存在する	sonzai suru
to expect (foresee)	見越す	mikosu
to explain (vt)	説明する	setsumei suru
to fall (vi)	落ちる	ochiru
to find (vt)	見つける	mitsukeru
to finish (vt)	終える	oeru
to fly (vi)	飛ぶ	tobu
to follow … (come after)	…について行く	… ni tsuiteiku
to forget (vi, vt)	忘れる	wasureru
to forgive (vt)	許す	yurusu
to give (vt)	手渡す	tewatasu
to give a hint	暗示する	anji suru
to go (on foot)	行く	iku
to go for a swim	海水浴をする	kaisuiyoku wo suru
to go out (from …)	出る	deru
to guess right	言い当てる	īateru
to have (vt)	持つ	motsu
to have breakfast	朝食をとる	chōshoku wo toru
to have dinner	夕食をとる	yūshoku wo toru
to have lunch	昼食をとる	chūshoku wo toru
to hear (vt)	聞く	kiku
to help (vt)	手伝う	tetsudau
to hide (vt)	隠す	kakusu
to hope (vi, vt)	希望する	kibō suru
to hunt (vi, vt)	狩る	karu
to hurry (vi)	急ぐ	isogu

15. The most important verbs. Part 3

to inform (vt)	知らせる	shiraseru
to insist (vi, vt)	主張する	shuchō suru

to insult (vt)	侮辱する	bujoku suru
to invite (vt)	招待する	shōtai suru
to joke (vi)	冗談を言う	jōdan wo iu
to keep (vt)	保つ	tamotsu
to keep silent	沈黙を守る	chinmoku wo mamoru
to kill (vt)	殺す	korosu
to know (sb)	知っている	shitte iru
to know (sth)	知る	shiru
to laugh (vi)	笑う	warau
to liberate (city, etc.)	解放する	kaihō suru
to like (I like ...)	好む	konomu
to look for ... (search)	探す	sagasu
to love (sb)	愛する	aisuru
to make a mistake	誤りをする	ayamari wo suru
to manage, to run	管理する	kanri suru
to mean (signify)	意味する	imi suru
to mention (talk about)	言及する	genkyū suru
to miss (school, etc.)	欠席する	kesseki suru
to notice (see)	見掛ける	mikakeru
to object (vi, vt)	反対する	hantai suru
to observe (see)	監視する	kanshi suru
to open (vt)	開ける	akeru
to order (meal, etc.)	注文する	chūmon suru
to order (mil.)	命令する	meirei suru
to own (possess)	所有する	shoyū suru
to participate (vi)	参加する	sanka suru
to pay (vi, vt)	払う	harau
to permit (vt)	許可する	kyoka suru
to plan (vt)	計画する	keikaku suru
to play (children)	遊ぶ	asobu
to pray (vi, vt)	祈る	inoru
to prefer (vt)	好む	konomu
to promise (vt)	約束する	yakusoku suru
to pronounce (vt)	発音する	hatsuon suru
to propose (vt)	提案する	teian suru
to punish (vt)	罰する	bassuru
to read (vi, vt)	読む	yomu
to recommend (vt)	推薦する	suisen suru
to refuse (vi, vt)	拒絶する	kyozetsu suru
to regret (be sorry)	後悔する	kōkai suru
to rent (sth from sb)	借りる	kariru
to repeat (say again)	復唱する	fukushō suru
to reserve, to book	予約する	yoyaku suru
to run (vi)	走る	hashiru

16. The most important verbs. Part 4

to save (rescue)	救出する	kyūshutsu suru
to say (~ thank you)	言う	iu
to scold (vt)	叱る［しかる］	shikaru
to see (vt)	見る	miru
to sell (vt)	売る	uru
to send (vt)	送る	okuru
to shoot (vi)	撃つ	utsu
to shout (vi)	叫ぶ	sakebu
to show (vt)	見せる	miseru
to sign (document)	署名する	shomei suru
to sit down (vi)	座る	suwaru
to smile (vi)	ほほえむ［微笑む］	hohoemu
to speak (vi, vt)	話す	hanasu
to steal (money, etc.)	盗む	nusumu
to stop (please ~ calling me)	止める	tomeru
to stop (for pause, etc.)	止まる	tomaru
to study (vt)	勉強する	benkyō suru
to swim (vi)	泳ぐ	oyogu
to take (vt)	取る	toru
to think (vi, vt)	思う	omō
to threaten (vt)	脅す	odosu
to touch (with hands)	触れる	fureru
to translate (vt)	翻訳する	honyaku suru
to trust (vt)	信用する	shinyō suru
to try (attempt)	試みる	kokoromiru
to turn (~ to the left)	曲がる	magaru
to underestimate (vt)	甘く見る	amaku miru
to understand (vt)	理解する	rikai suru
to unite (vt)	合体させる	gattai saseru
to wait (vt)	待つ	matsu
to want (wish, desire)	欲する	hossuru
to warn (vt)	警告する	keikoku suru
to work (vi)	働く	hataraku
to write (vt)	書く	kaku
to write down	書き留める	kakitomeru

TIME. CALENDAR

17. Weekdays

Monday	月曜日	getsuyōbi
Tuesday	火曜日	kayōbi
Wednesday	水曜日	suiyōbi
Thursday	木曜日	mokuyōbi
Friday	金曜日	kinyōbi
Saturday	土曜日	doyōbi
Sunday	日曜日	nichiyōbi
today (adv)	今日	kyō
tomorrow (adv)	明日	ashita
the day after tomorrow	明後日 ［あさって］	asatte
yesterday (adv)	昨日	kinō
the day before yesterday	一昨日 ［おととい］	ototoi
day	日	nichi
working day	営業日	eigyōbi
public holiday	公休	kōkyū
day off	休み	yasumi
weekend	週末	shūmatsu
all day long	一日中	ichi nichi chū
next day (adv)	翌日	yokujitsu
two days ago	2日前に	futsu ka mae ni
the day before	その前日に	sono zenjitsu ni
daily (adj)	毎日の	mainichi no
every day (adv)	毎日	mainichi
week	週	shū
last week (adv)	先週	senshū
next week (adv)	来週	raishū
weekly (adj)	毎週の	maishū no
every week (adv)	毎週	maishū
twice a week	週に2回	shūni nikai
every Tuesday	毎週火曜日	maishū kayōbi

18. Hours. Day and night

morning	朝	asa
in the morning	朝に	asa ni
noon, midday	正午	shōgo

in the afternoon	午後に	gogo ni
evening	夕方	yūgata
in the evening	夕方に	yūgata ni
night	夜	yoru
at night	夜に	yoru ni
midnight	真夜中	mayonaka
second	秒	byō
minute	分	fun, pun
hour	時間	jikan
half an hour	30分	san jū fun
quarter of an hour	15分	jū go fun
fifteen minutes	15分	jū go fun
24 hours	一昼夜	icchūya
sunrise	日の出	hinode
dawn	夜明け	yoake
early morning	早朝	sōchō
sunset	夕日	yūhi
early in the morning	早朝に	sōchō ni
this morning	今朝	kesa
tomorrow morning	明日の朝	ashita no asa
this afternoon	今日の午後	kyō no gogo
in the afternoon	午後	gogo
tomorrow afternoon	明日の午後	ashita no gogo
tonight (this evening)	今夜	konya
tomorrow night	明日の夜	ashita no yoru
at 3 o'clock sharp	3時ちょうどに	sanji chōdo ni
about 4 o'clock	4時頃	yoji goro
by 12 o'clock	12時までに	jūniji made ni
in 20 minutes	20分後	nijuppungo
in an hour	一時間後	ichi jikan go
on time (adv)	予定通りに	yotei dōri ni
a quarter of ...	…時15分	… ji jyūgo fun
within an hour	1時間で	ichi jikan de
every 15 minutes	15分ごとに	jyūgo fun goto ni
round the clock	昼も夜も	hiru mo yoru mo

19. Months. Seasons

January	一月	ichigatsu
February	二月	nigatsu
March	三月	sangatsu
April	四月	shigatsu

May	五月	gogatsu
June	六月	rokugatsu
July	七月	shichigatsu
August	八月	hachigatsu
September	九月	kugatsu
October	十月	jūgatsu
November	十一月	jūichigatsu
December	十二月	jūnigatsu
spring	春	haru
in spring	春に	haru ni
spring (as adj)	春の	haru no
summer	夏	natsu
in summer	夏に	natsu ni
summer (as adj)	夏の	natsu no
fall	秋	aki
in fall	秋に	aki ni
fall (as adj)	秋の	aki no
winter	冬	fuyu
in winter	冬に	fuyu ni
winter (as adj)	冬の	fuyu no
month	月	tsuki
this month	今月	kongetsu
next month	来月	raigetsu
last month	先月	sengetsu
a month ago	一ヶ月前	ichi kagetsu mae
in a month	一ヶ月後	ichi kagetsu go
in two months	二ヶ月後	ni kagetsu go
the whole month	丸一ヶ月	maru ichi kagetsu
all month long	一ヶ月間ずっと	ichi kagetsu kan zutto
monthly (~ magazine)	月刊の	gekkan no
monthly (adv)	毎月	maitsuki
every month	月1回	tsuki ichi kai
twice a month	月に2回	tsuki ni ni kai
year	年	nen
this year	今年	kotoshi
next year	来年	rainen
last year	去年	kyonen
a year ago	一年前	ichi nen mae
in a year	一年後	ichi nen go
in two years	二年後	ni nen go
the whole year	丸一年	maru ichi nen
all year long	通年	tsūnen

every year	毎年	maitoshi
annual (adj)	毎年の	maitoshi no
annually (adv)	年1回	toshi ichi kai
4 times a year	年に4回	

date (e.g., today's ~)	日付	hizuke
date (e.g., ~ of birth)	年月日	nengappi
calendar	カレンダー	karendā

| half a year | 半年 | hantoshi |
| six months | 6ヶ月 | |

| season (summer, etc.) | 季節 | kisetsu |
| century | 世紀 | seiki |

TRAVEL. HOTEL

20. Trip. Travel

tourism	観光	kankō
tourist	観光客	kankō kyaku
trip, voyage	旅行	ryokō

adventure	冒険	bōken
trip, journey	旅	tabi

vacation	休暇	kyūka
to be on vacation	休暇中です	kyūka chū desu
rest	休み	yasumi

train	列車	ressha
by train	列車で	ressha de
airplane	航空機	kōkūki
by airplane	飛行機で	hikōki de

by car	車で	kuruma de
by ship	船で	fune de

luggage	荷物	nimotsu
suitcase, luggage	スーツケース	sūtsukēsu
luggage cart	荷物カート	nimotsu kāto

passport	パスポート	pasupōto
visa	ビザ	biza

ticket	乗車券	jōsha ken
air ticket	航空券	kōkū ken

guidebook	ガイドブック	gaido bukku
map	地図	chizu

area (rural ~)	地域	chīki
place, site	場所	basho

exotic (n)	エキゾチック	ekizochikku
exotic (adj)	エキゾチックな	ekizochikku na
amazing (adj)	驚くべき	odoroku beki

group	団	dan
excursion	小旅行	shō ryokō
guide (person)	ツアーガイド	tuā gaido

21. Hotel

hotel	ホテル	hoteru
motel	モーテル	mō teru
three-star	三つ星	mitsu boshi
five-star	五つ星	itsutsu boshi
to stay (in hotel, etc.)	泊まる	tomaru
room	部屋、ルーム	heya, rūmu
single room	シングルルーム	shinguru rūmu
double room	ダブルルーム	daburu rūmu
to book a room	部屋を予約する	heya wo yoyaku suru
half board	ハーフボード	hāfu bōdo
full board	フルボード	furu bōdo
with bath	浴槽付きの	yokusō tsuki no
with shower	シャワー付きの	shawā tsuki no
satellite television	衛星テレビ	eisei terebi
air-conditioner	エアコン	eakon
towel	タオル	taoru
key	鍵	kagi
administrator	管理人	kanri jin
chambermaid	客室係	kyakushitsu gakari
porter, bellboy	ベルボーイ	beru bōi
doorman	ドアマン	doa man
restaurant	レストラン	resutoran
pub, bar	パブ、バー	pabu, bā
breakfast	朝食	chōshoku
dinner	夕食	yūshoku
buffet	ビュッフェ	byuffe
lobby	ロビー	robī
elevator	エレベーター	erebētā
DO NOT DISTURB	起こさないで下さい	okosa nai de kudasai
NO SMOKING	禁煙	kinen

22. Sightseeing

monument	記念碑	kinen hi
fortress	要塞	yōsai
palace	宮殿	kyūden
castle	城	shiro
tower	塔	tō
mausoleum	マウソレウム	mausoreumu

architecture	建築	kenchiku
medieval (adj)	中世の	chūsei no
ancient (adj)	古代の	kodai no
national (adj)	国の	kuni no
well-known (adj)	有名な	yūmei na

tourist	観光客	kankō kyaku
guide (person)	ガイド	gaido
excursion, guided tour	小旅行	shō ryokō
to show (vt)	案内する	annai suru
to tell (vt)	話をする	hanashi wo suru

to find (vt)	見つける	mitsukeru
to get lost (lose one's way)	道に迷う	michi ni mayō
map (e.g., subway ~)	地図	chizu
map (e.g., city ~)	地図	chizu

souvenir, gift	土産	miyage
gift shop	土産品店	miyage hin ten
to take pictures	写真に撮る	shashin ni toru
to be photographed	写真を撮られる	shashin wo torareru

TRANSPORTATION

23. Airport

airport	空港	kūkō
airplane	航空機	kōkūki
airline	航空会社	kōkū gaisha
air-traffic controller	航空管制官	kōkū kansei kan
departure	出発	shuppatsu
arrival	到着	tōchaku
to arrive (by plane)	到着する	tōchaku suru
departure time	出発時刻	shuppatsu jikoku
arrival time	到着時刻	tōchaku jikoku
to be delayed	遅れる	okureru
flight delay	フライトの遅延	furaito no chien
information board	フライト情報	furaito jōhō
information	案内	annai
to announce (vt)	アナウンスする	anaunsu suru
flight (e.g., next ~)	フライト	furaito
customs	税関	zeikan
customs officer	税関吏	zeikanri
customs declaration	税関申告	zeikan shinkoku
to fill out (vt)	記入する	kinyū suru
to fill out the declaration	申告書を記入する	shinkoku sho wo kinyū suru
passport control	入国審査	nyūkoku shinsa
luggage	荷物	nimotsu
hand luggage	持ち込み荷物	mochikomi nimotsu
Lost Luggage Desk	荷物紛失窓口	nimotsu funshitsu madoguchi
luggage cart	荷物カート	nimotsu kāto
landing	着陸	chakuriku
landing strip	滑走路	kassō ro
to land (vi)	着陸する	chakuriku suru
airstairs	タラップ	tarappu
check-in	チェックイン	chekkuin
check-in desk	チェックインカウンター	chekkuin kauntā

to check-in (vi)	チェックインする	chekkuin suru
boarding pass	搭乗券	tōjō ken
departure gate	出発ゲート	shuppatsu gēto
transit	乗り継ぎ	noritsugi
to wait (vt)	待つ	matsu
departure lounge	出発ロビー	shuppatsu robī
to see off	見送る	miokuru
to say goodbye	別れを告げる	wakare wo tsugeru

24. Airplane

airplane	航空機	kōkūki
air ticket	航空券	kōkū ken
airline	航空会社	kōkū gaisha
airport	空港	kūkō
supersonic (adj)	超音速の	chō onsoku no
captain	機長	kichō
crew	乗務員	jōmu in
pilot	パイロット	pairotto
flight attendant	客室乗務員	kyakushitsu jōmu in
navigator	航空士	kōkū shi
wings	翼	tsubasa
tail	尾部	o bu
cockpit	コックピット	kokkupitto
engine	エンジン	enjin
undercarriage	着陸装置	chakuriku sōchi
turbine	タービン	tābin
propeller	プロペラ	puropera
black box	ブラックボックス	burakku bokkusu
control column	操縦ハンドル	sōjū handoru
fuel	燃料	nenryō
safety card	安全のしおり	anzen no shiori
oxygen mask	酸素マスク	sanso masuku
uniform	制服	seifuku
life vest	ライフジャケット	raifu jaketto
parachute	落下傘	rakkasan
takeoff	離陸	ririku
to take off (vi)	離陸する	ririku suru
runway	滑走路	kassō ro
visibility	視程	shitei
flight (act of flying)	飛行	hikō
altitude	高度	kōdo
air pocket	エアポケット	eapoketto

seat	席	seki
headphones	ヘッドホン	heddohon
folding tray	折りたたみ式のテーブル	oritatami shiki no tēburu
airplane window	機窓	kisō
aisle	通路	tsūro

25. Train

train	列車	ressha
suburban train	通勤列車	tsūkin ressha
express train	高速鉄道	kōsoku tetsudō
diesel locomotive	ディーゼル機関車	dīzeru kikan sha
steam engine	蒸気機関車	jōki kikan sha

| passenger car | 客車 | kyakusha |
| dining car | 食堂車 | shokudō sha |

rails	レール	rēru
railroad	鉄道	tetsudō
railway tie	枕木	makuragi

platform (railway ~)	ホーム	hōmu
track (~ 1, 2, etc.)	線路	senro
semaphore	鉄道信号機	tetsudō shingō ki
station	駅	eki

engineer	機関士	kikan shi
porter (of luggage)	ポーター	pōtā
train steward	車掌	shashō
passenger	乗客	jōkyaku
conductor	検札係	kensatsu gakari

| corridor (in train) | 通路 | tsūro |
| emergency break | 非常ブレーキ | hijō burēki |

compartment	コンパートメント	konpātomento
berth	寝台	shindai
upper berth	上段寝台	jōdan shindai
lower berth	下段寝台	gedan shindai
bed linen	リネン	rinen

ticket	乗車券	jōsha ken
schedule	時刻表	jikoku hyō
information display	発車標	hassha shirube

to leave, to depart	発車する	hassha suru
departure (of train)	発車	hassha
to arrive (ab. train)	到着する	tōchaku suru
arrival	到着	tōchaku
to arrive by train	電車で来る	densha de kuru

to get on the train	電車に乗る	densha ni noru
to get off the train	電車をおりる	densha wo oriru
train wreck	鉄道事故	tetsudō jiko
to be derailed	脱線する	dassen suru
steam engine	蒸気機関車	jōki kikan sha
stoker, fireman	火夫	kafu
firebox	火室	kashitsu
coal	石炭	sekitan

26. Ship

ship	船舶	senpaku
vessel	大型船	ōgata sen
steamship	蒸気船	jōki sen
riverboat	川船	kawabune
ocean liner	遠洋定期船	enyō teiki sen
cruiser	クルーザー	kurūzā
yacht	ヨット	yotto
tugboat	曳船	eisen
barge	艀、バージ	hashike, bāji
ferry	フェリー	ferī
sailing ship	帆船	hansen
brigantine	ブリガンティン	burigantin
ice breaker	砕水船	saihyō sen
submarine	潜水艦	sensui kan
boat (flat-bottomed ~)	ボート	bōto
dinghy	ディンギー	dingī
lifeboat	救命艇	kyūmei tei
motorboat	モーターボート	mōtābōto
captain	船長	senchō
seaman	船員	senin
sailor	水夫	suifu
crew	乗組員	norikumi in
boatswain	ボースン	bōsun
ship's boy	キャビンボーイ	kyabin bōi
cook	船のコック	fune no kokku
ship's doctor	船医	seni
deck	甲板	kanpan
mast	マスト	masuto
sail	帆	ho
hold	船倉	funagura

bow (prow)	船首	senshu
stern	船尾	senbi
oar	櫂	kai
screw propeller	プロペラ	puropera
cabin	船室	senshitsu
wardroom	士官室	shikan shitsu
engine room	機関室	kikan shitsu
bridge	船橋	funabashi
radio room	無線室	musen shitsu
wave (radio)	電波	denpa
logbook	航海日誌	kōkai nisshi
spyglass	単眼望遠鏡	tangan bōenkyō
bell	船鐘	funekane
flag	旗	hata
rope (mooring ~)	ロープ	rōpu
knot (bowline, etc.)	結び目	musubime
deckrail	手摺	tesuri
gangway	舷門	genmon
anchor	錨 [いかり]	ikari
to weigh anchor	錨をあげる	ikari wo ageru
to drop anchor	錨を下ろす	ikari wo orosu
anchor chain	錨鎖	byōsa
port (harbor)	港	minato
berth, wharf	埠頭	futō
to berth (moor)	係留する	keiryū suru
to cast off	出航する	shukkō suru
trip, voyage	旅行	ryokō
cruise (sea trip)	クルーズ	kurūzu
course (route)	針路	shinro
route (itinerary)	船のルート	fune no rūto
fairway	航路	kōro
shallows (shoal)	浅瀬	asase
to run aground	浅瀬に乗り上げる	asase ni noriageru
storm	嵐	arashi
signal	信号	shingō
to sink (vi)	沈没する	chinbotsu suru
Man overboard!	落水したぞ！	ochimizu shi ta zo!
SOS	SOS	
ring buoy	救命浮輪	kyūmei ukiwa

CITY

27. Urban transportation

bus	バス	basu
streetcar	路面電車	romen densha
trolley	トロリーバス	tororībasu
route (of bus)	路線	rosen
number (e.g., bus ~)	番号	bangō
to go by ...	…で行く	... de iku
to get on (~ the bus)	乗る	noru
to get off ...	降りる	oriru
stop (e.g., bus ~)	停	toma
next stop	次の停車駅	tsugi no teishaeki
terminus	終着駅	shūchakueki
schedule	時刻表	jikoku hyō
to wait (vt)	待つ	matsu
ticket	乗車券	jōsha ken
fare	運賃	unchin
cashier (ticket seller)	販売員	hanbai in
ticket inspection	集札	shū satsu
conductor	車掌	shashō
to be late (for ...)	遅れる	okureru
to miss (~ the train, etc.)	逃す	nogasu
to be in a hurry	急ぐ	isogu
taxi, cab	タクシー	takushī
taxi driver	タクシーの運転手	takushī no unten shu
by taxi	タクシーで	takushī de
taxi stand	タクシー乗り場	takushī noriba
to call a taxi	タクシーを呼ぶ	takushī wo yobu
to take a taxi	タクシーに乗る	takushī ni noru
traffic	交通	kōtsū
traffic jam	渋滞	jūtai
rush hour	ラッシュアワー	rasshuawā
to park (vi)	駐車する	chūsha suru
to park (vt)	駐車する	chūsha suru
parking lot	駐車場	chūsha jō
subway	地下鉄	chikatetsu
station	駅	eki

to take the subway	地下鉄で行く	chikatetsu de iku
train	列車	ressha
train station	鉄道駅	tetsudō eki

28. City. Life in the city

city, town	市、町	shi, machi
capital city	首都	shuto
village	村	mura

city map	市街地図	shigai chizu
downtown	中心街	chūshin gai
suburb	郊外	kōgai
suburban (adj)	郊外の	kōgai no

outskirts	町外れ	machihazure
environs (suburbs)	近郊	kinkō
city block	街区	gaiku
residential block	住宅街	jūtaku gai

traffic	交通	kōtsū
traffic lights	信号	shingō
public transportation	公共交通機関	kōkyō kōtsū kikan
intersection	交差点	kōsaten

crosswalk	横断歩道	ōdan hodō
pedestrian underpass	地下道	chikadō
to cross (vt)	横断する	ōdan suru
pedestrian	歩行者	hokō sha
sidewalk	歩道	hodō

bridge	橋	hashi
bank (riverbank)	堤防	teibō
fountain	噴水	funsui

allée	散歩道	sanpomichi
park	公園	kōen
boulevard	大通り	ōdōri
square	広場	hiroba
avenue (wide street)	アヴェニュー	avenyū
street	通り	tōri
side street	わき道 [脇道]	wakimichi
dead end	行き止まり	ikidomari

house	家屋	kaoku
building	建物	tatemono
skyscraper	摩天楼	matenrō

| facade | ファサード | fasādo |
| roof | 屋根 | yane |

window	窓	mado
arch	アーチ	āchi
column	柱	hashira
corner	角	kado

store window	ショーウインドー	shōuindō
store sign	店看板	mise kanban
poster	ポスター	posutā
advertising poster	広告ポスター	kōkoku posutā
billboard	広告掲示板	kōkoku keijiban

garbage, trash	ゴミ［ごみ］	gomi
garbage can	ゴミ入れ	gomi ire
to litter (vi)	ゴミを投げ捨てる	gomi wo nagesuteru
garbage dump	ゴミ捨て場	gomi suteba

phone booth	電話ボックス	denwa bokkusu
lamppost	街灯柱	gaitō bashira
bench (park ~)	ベンチ	benchi

police officer	警官	keikan
police	警察	keisatsu
beggar	こじき	kojiki
homeless, bum	ホームレス	hōmuresu

29. Urban institutions

store	店、…屋	mise, …ya
drugstore, pharmacy	薬局	yakkyoku
optical store	眼鏡店	megane ten
shopping mall	ショッピングモール	shoppingu mōru
supermarket	スーパーマーケット	sūpāmāketto

bakery	パン屋	panya
baker	パン職人	pan shokunin
candy store	菓子店	kashi ten
grocery store	食料品店	shokuryō hin ten
butcher shop	肉屋	nikuya

| produce store | 八百屋 | yaoya |
| market | 市場 | ichiba |

coffee house	喫茶店	kissaten
restaurant	レストラン	resutoran
pub	パブ	pabu
pizzeria	ピザ屋	piza ya

hair salon	美容院	biyō in
post office	郵便局	yūbin kyoku
dry cleaners	クリーニング屋	kurīningu ya

photo studio	写真館	shashin kan
shoe store	靴屋	kutsuya
bookstore	本屋	honya
sporting goods store	スポーツ店	supōtsu ten
clothes repair	洋服直し専門店	yōfuku naoshi senmon ten
formal wear rental	貸衣裳店	kashi ishō ten
movie rental store	レンタルビデオ店	rentarubideo ten
circus	サーカス	sākasu
zoo	動物園	dōbutsu en
movie theater	映画館	eiga kan
museum	博物館	hakubutsukan
library	図書館	toshokan
theater	劇場	gekijō
opera	オペラハウス	opera hausu
nightclub	ナイトクラブ	naito kurabu
casino	カジノ	kajino
mosque	モスク	mosuku
synagogue	シナゴーグ	shinagōgu
cathedral	大聖堂	dai seidō
temple	寺院	jīn
church	教会	kyōkai
college	大学	daigaku
university	大学	daigaku
school	学校	gakkō
prefecture	県庁舎	ken chōsha
city hall	市役所	shiyaku sho
hotel	ホテル	hoteru
bank	銀行	ginkō
embassy	大使館	taishikan
travel agency	旅行代理店	ryokō dairi ten
information office	案内所	annai sho
money exchange	両替所	ryōgae sho
subway	地下鉄	chikatetsu
hospital	病院	byōin
gas station	ガソリンスタンド	gasorin sutando
parking lot	駐車場	chūsha jō

30. Signs

store sign	店看板	mise kanban
notice (written text)	看板	kanban

poster	ポスター	posutā
direction sign	方向看板	hōkō kanban
arrow (sign)	矢印	yajirushi
caution	注意	chūi
warning sign	警告表示	keikoku hyōji
to warn (vt)	警告する	keikoku suru
day off	定休日	teikyū bi
timetable (schedule)	営業時間の看板	eigyō jikan no kanban
opening hours	営業時間	eigyō jikan
WELCOME!	ようこそ	yōkoso
ENTRANCE	入口	iriguchi
EXIT	出口	deguchi
PUSH	押す	osu
PULL	引く	hiku
OPEN	営業中	eigyō chū
CLOSED	休業日	kyūgyōbi
WOMEN	女性	josei
MEN	男性	dansei
DISCOUNTS	割引	waribiki
SALE	バーゲンセール	bāgen sēru
NEW!	新発売！	shin hatsubai!
FREE	無料	muryō
ATTENTION!	ご注意！	go chūi!
NO VACANCIES	満室	manshitsu
RESERVED	御予約席	go yoyaku seki
ADMINISTRATION	支配人	shihainin
STAFF ONLY	関係者以外立入禁止	kankei sha igai tachīrikinshi
BEWARE OF THE DOG!	猛犬注意	mōken chūi
NO SMOKING	禁煙	kinen
DO NOT TOUCH!	手を触れるな	te wo fureru na
DANGEROUS	危険	kiken
DANGER	危険	kiken
HIGH TENSION	高電圧	kō denatsu
NO SWIMMING!	水泳禁止	suiei kinshi
OUT OF ORDER	故障中	koshō chū
FLAMMABLE	可燃性物質	kanen sei busshitsu
FORBIDDEN	禁止	kinshi
NO TRESPASSING!	通り抜け禁止	tōrinuke kinshi
WET PAINT	ペンキ塗りたて	penki nuritate

31. Shopping

to buy (purchase)	買う	kau
purchase	買い物	kaimono
to go shopping	買い物に行く	kaimono ni iku
shopping	ショッピング	shoppingu
to be open (ab. store)	開いている	hiraite iru
to be closed	閉まっている	shimatte iru
footwear	履物	hakimono
clothes, clothing	洋服	yōfuku
cosmetics	化粧品	keshō hin
food products	食料品	shokuryō hin
gift, present	土産	miyage
salesman	店員、売り子	tenin, uriko
saleswoman	店員、売り子	tenin, uriko
check out, cash desk	レジ	reji
mirror	鏡	kagami
counter (in shop)	カウンター	kauntā
fitting room	試着室	shichaku shitsu
to try on	試着する	shichaku suru
to fit (ab. dress, etc.)	合う	au
to like (I like ...)	好む	konomu
price	価格	kakaku
price tag	値札	nefuda
to cost (vt)	かかる	kakaru
How much?	いくら?	ikura ?
discount	割引	waribiki
inexpensive (adj)	安価な	anka na
cheap (adj)	安い	yasui
expensive (adj)	高い	takai
It's expensive	それは高い	sore wa takai
rental (n)	レンタル	rentaru
to rent (~ a tuxedo)	レンタルする	rentaru suru
credit	信用取引	shinyō torihiki
on credit (adv)	付けで	tsuke de

CLOTHING & ACCESSORIES

32. Outerwear. Coats

clothes	洋服	yōfuku
outer clothes	上着	uwagi
winter clothes	冬服	fuyu fuku
overcoat	オーバーコート	ōbā kōto
fur coat	毛皮のコート	kegawa no kōto
fur jacket	毛皮のジャケット	kegawa no jaketto
down coat	ダウンコート	daun kōto
jacket (e.g., leather ~)	ジャケット	jaketto
raincoat	レインコート	reinkōto
waterproof (adj)	防水の	bōsui no

33. Men's & women's clothing

shirt	ワイシャツ	waishatsu
pants	ズボン	zubon
jeans	ジーンズ	jīnzu
jacket (of man's suit)	ジャケット	jaketto
suit	背広	sebiro
dress (frock)	ドレス	doresu
skirt	スカート	sukāto
blouse	ブラウス	burausu
knitted jacket	ニットジャケット	nitto jaketto
jacket (of woman's suit)	ジャケット	jaketto
T-shirt	Tシャツ	tīshatsu
shorts (short trousers)	半ズボン	han zubon
tracksuit	トラックスーツ	torakku sūtsu
bathrobe	バスローブ	basurōbu
pajamas	パジャマ	pajama
sweater	セーター	sētā
pullover	プルオーバー	puruōbā
vest	ベスト	besuto
tailcoat	燕尾服	enbifuku
tuxedo	タキシード	takishīdo
uniform	制服	seifuku

workwear	作業服	sagyō fuku
overalls	オーバーオール	ōbā ōru
coat (e.g., doctor's smock)	コート	kōto

34. Clothing. Underwear

underwear	下着	shitagi
boxers	ボクサーパンツ	bokusā pantsu
panties	パンティー	pantī
undershirt (A-shirt)	タンクトップ	tanku toppu
socks	靴下	kutsushita
nightgown	ネグリジェ	negurije
bra	ブラジャー	burajā
knee highs	ニーソックス	nīsokkusu
tights	パンティストッキング	pantī sutokkingu
stockings (thigh highs)	ストッキング	sutokkingu
bathing suit	水着	mizugi

35. Headwear

hat	帽子	bōshi
fedora	フェドーラ帽	fedōra bō
baseball cap	野球帽	yakyū bō
flatcap	ハンチング帽	hanchingu bō
beret	ベレー帽	berē bō
hood	フード	fūdo
panama hat	パナマ帽	panama bō
knitted hat	ニット帽	nitto bō
headscarf	ヘッドスカーフ	heddo sukāfu
women's hat	婦人帽子	fujin bōshi
hard hat	安全ヘルメット	anzen herumetto
garrison cap	略帽	rya ku bō
helmet	ヘルメット	herumetto
derby	山高帽	yamataka bō
top hat	シルクハット	shiruku hatto

36. Footwear

footwear	靴	kutsu
ankle boots	アンクルブーツ	ankuru būtsu
shoes (low-heeled ~)	パンプス	panpusu

boots (cowboy ~)	ブーツ	būtsu
slippers	スリッパ	surippa
tennis shoes	テニスシューズ	tenisu shūzu
sneakers	スニーカー	sunīkā
sandals	サンダル	sandaru
cobbler	靴修理屋	kutsu shūri ya
heel	かかと [踵]	kakato
pair (of shoes)	靴一足	kutsu issoku
shoestring	靴ひも	kutsu himo
to lace (vt)	靴ひもを結ぶ	kutsu himo wo musubu
shoehorn	靴べら	kutsubera
shoe polish	靴クリーム	kutsu kurīmu

37. Personal accessories

gloves	手袋	tebukuro
mittens	ミトン	miton
scarf (muffler)	マフラー	mafurā
glasses	めがね [眼鏡]	megane
frame (eyeglass ~)	めがねのふち	megane no fuchi
umbrella	傘	kasa
walking stick	杖	tsue
hairbrush	ヘアブラシ	hea burashi
fan	扇子	sensu
necktie	ネクタイ	nekutai
bow tie	蝶ネクタイ	chō nekutai
suspenders	サスペンダー	sasupendā
handkerchief	ハンカチ	hankachi
comb	くし [櫛]	kushi
barrette	髪留め	kami tome
hairpin	ヘアピン	hea pin
buckle	バックル	bakkuru
belt	ベルト	beruto
shoulder strap	ショルダーベルト	shorudā beruto
bag (handbag)	バッグ	baggu
purse	ハンドバッグ	hando baggu
backpack	バックパック	bakku pakku

38. Clothing. Miscellaneous

fashion	ファッション	fasshon
in vogue (adj)	流行の	ryūkō no

fashion designer	ファッションデザイナー	fasshon dezainā
collar	襟	eri
pocket	ポケット	poketto
pocket (as adj)	ポケットの	poketto no
sleeve	袖	sode
hanging loop	ハンガーループ	hangā rūpu
fly (on trousers)	ズボンのファスナー	zubon no fasunā
zipper (fastener)	チャック	chakku
fastener	ファスナー	fasunā
button	ボタン	botan
buttonhole	ボタンの穴	botan no ana
to come off (ab. button)	取れる	toreru
to sew (vi, vt)	縫う	nū
to embroider (vi, vt)	刺繍する	shishū suru
embroidery	刺繍	shishū
sewing needle	縫い針	nui bari
thread	糸	ito
seam	縫い目	nuime
to get dirty (vi)	汚れる	yogoreru
stain (mark, spot)	染み	shimi
to crease, crumple (vi)	しわになる	shiwa ni naru
to tear (vt)	引き裂く	hikisaku
clothes moth	コイガ	koi ga

39. Personal care. Cosmetics

toothpaste	歯磨き粉	hamigakiko
toothbrush	歯ブラシ	haburashi
to brush one's teeth	歯を磨く	ha wo migaku
razor	カミソリ［剃刀］	kamisori
shaving cream	シェービングクリーム	shēbingu kurīmu
to shave (vi)	ひげを剃る	hige wo soru
soap	せっけん［石鹸］	sekken
shampoo	シャンプー	shanpū
scissors	はさみ	hasami
nail file	爪やすり	tsume yasuri
nail clippers	爪切り	tsume giri
tweezers	ピンセット	pinsetto
cosmetics	化粧品	keshō hin
face mask	フェイスパック	feisu pakku
manicure	マニキュア	manikyua
to have a manicure	マニキュアをしてもらう	manikyua wo shi te morau
pedicure	ペディキュア	pedikyua

make-up bag	化粧ポーチ	keshō pōchi
face powder	フェイスパウダー	feisu pauda
powder compact	ファンデーション	fandēshon
blusher	チーク	chīku

perfume (bottled)	香水	kōsui
toilet water (perfume)	オードトワレ	ōdotoware
lotion	ローション	rō shon
cologne	オーデコロン	ōdekoron

eyeshadow	アイシャドウ	aishadō
eyeliner	アイライナー	airainā
mascara	マスカラ	masukara

lipstick	口紅	kuchibeni
nail polish, enamel	ネイルポリッシュ	neiru porisshu
hair spray	ヘアスプレー	hea supurē
deodorant	デオドラント	deodoranto

cream	クリーム	kurīmu
face cream	フェイスクリーム	feisu kurīmu
hand cream	ハンドクリーム	hando kurīmu
anti-wrinkle cream	しわ取りクリーム	shiwa tori kurīmu
day cream	昼用クリーム	hiruyō kurīmu
night cream	夜用クリーム	yoruyō kurīmu
day (as adj)	昼用…	hiruyō …
night (as adj)	夜用…	yoruyō …

tampon	タンポン	tanpon
toilet paper	トイレットペーパー	toiretto pēpā
hair dryer	ヘアドライヤー	hea doraiyā

40. Watches. Clocks

watch (wristwatch)	時計	tokei
dial	ダイヤル	daiyaru
hand (of clock, watch)	針	hari
metal watch band	金属ベルト	kinzoku beruto
watch strap	腕時計バンド	udedokei bando

battery	電池	denchi
to be dead (battery)	切れる	kireru
to change a battery	電池を交換する	denchi wo kōkan suru
to run fast	進んでいる	susundeiru
to run slow	遅れている	okureteiru

wall clock	掛け時計	kakedokei
hourglass	砂時計	sunadokei
sundial	日時計	hidokei
alarm clock	目覚まし時計	mezamashi dokei

| watchmaker | 時計職人 | tokei shokunin |
| to repair (vt) | 修理する | shūri suru |

EVERYDAY EXPERIENCE

41. Money

money	お金	okane
currency exchange	両替	ryōgae
exchange rate	為替レート	kawase rēto
ATM	ATM	ētīemu
coin	コイン	koin
dollar	ドル	doru
euro	ユーロ	yūro
lira	リラ	rira
Deutschmark	ドイツマルク	doitsu maruku
franc	フラン	furan
pound sterling	スターリング・ポンド	sutāringu pondo
yen	円	en
debt	債務	saimu
debtor	債務者	saimu sha
to lend (money)	貸す	kasu
to borrow (vi, vt)	借りる	kariru
bank	銀行	ginkō
account	口座	kōza
to deposit (vt)	預金する	yokin suru
to deposit into the account	口座に預金する	kōza ni yokin suru
to withdraw (vt)	引き出す	hikidasu
credit card	クレジットカード	kurejitto kādo
cash	現金	genkin
check	小切手	kogitte
to write a check	小切手を書く	kogitte wo kaku
checkbook	小切手帳	kogitte chō
wallet	財布	saifu
change purse	小銭入れ	kozeni ire
billfold	札入れ	satsu ire
safe	金庫	kinko
heir	相続人	sōzokunin
inheritance	相続	sōzoku
fortune (wealth)	財産	zaisan
lease, rent	賃貸	chintai
rent money	家賃	yachin

to rent (sth from sb)	借りる	kariru
price	価格	kakaku
cost	費用	hiyō
sum	合計金額	gōkei kingaku

to spend (vt)	お金を使う	okane wo tsukau
expenses	出費	shuppi
to economize (vi, vt)	倹約する	kenyaku suru
economical	節約の	setsuyaku no

to pay (vi, vt)	払う	harau
payment	支払い	shiharai
change (give the ~)	おつり	o tsuri

tax	税	zei
fine	罰金	bakkin
to fine (vt)	罰金を科す	bakkin wo kasu

42. Post. Postal service

post office	郵便局	yūbin kyoku
mail (letters, etc.)	郵便物	yūbin butsu
mailman	郵便配達人	yūbin haitatsu jin
opening hours	営業時間	eigyō jikan

letter	手紙	tegami
registered letter	書留郵便	kakitome yūbin
postcard	はがき［葉書］	hagaki
telegram	電報	denpō
parcel	小包	kozutsumi
money transfer	送金	sōkin

to receive (vt)	受け取る	uketoru
to send (vt)	送る	okuru
sending	送信	sōshin

address	住所	jūsho
ZIP code	郵便番号	yūbin bangō
sender	送り主	okurinushi
receiver, addressee	受取人	uketorinin

| name | 名前 | namae |
| family name | 姓 | sei |

rate (of postage)	郵便料金	yūbin ryōkin
standard (adj)	通常の	tsūjō no
economical (adj)	エコノミー航空	ekonomīkōkū

| weight | 重さ | omo sa |
| to weigh up (vt) | 量る | hakaru |

envelope	封筒	fūtō
postage stamp	郵便切手	yūbin kitte
to stamp an envelope	封筒に切手を貼る	fūtō ni kitte wo haru

43. Banking

| bank | 銀行 | ginkō |
| branch (of bank, etc.) | 支店 | shiten |

| bank clerk, consultant | 銀行員 | ginkōin |
| manager (director) | 長 | chō |

banking account	口座	kōza
account number	口座番号	kōza bangō
checking account	当座預金口座	tōza yokin kōza
savings account	貯蓄預金口座	chochiku yokin kōza

| to open an account | 口座を開く | kōza wo hiraku |
| to close the account | 口座を解約する | kōza wo kaiyaku suru |

| to deposit into the account | 口座に預金する | kōza ni yokin suru |
| to withdraw (vt) | 引き出す | hikidasu |

| deposit | 預金 | yokin |
| to make a deposit | 預金する | yokin suru |

| wire transfer | 送金 | sōkin |
| to wire, to transfer | 送金する | sōkin suru |

| sum | 合計金額 | gōkei kingaku |
| How much? | いくら？ | ikura ? |

| signature | 署名 | shomei |
| to sign (vt) | 署名する | shomei suru |

| credit card | クレジットカード | kurejitto kādo |
| code | コード | kōdo |

| credit card number | クレジットカード番号 | kurejitto kādo bangō |
| ATM | ATM | ētīemu |

check	小切手	kogitte
to write a check	小切手を書く	kogitte wo kaku
checkbook	小切手帳	kogitte chō

loan (bank ~)	融資	yūshi
to apply for a loan	融資を申し込む	yūshi wo mōshikomu
to get a loan	融資を受ける	yūshi wo ukeru
to give a loan	融資を行う	yūshi wo okonau
guarantee	保障	hoshō

44. Telephone. Phone conversation

telephone	電話	denwa
mobile phone	携帯電話	keitai denwa
answering machine	留守番電話	rusuban denwa
to call (telephone)	電話する	denwa suru
phone call	電話	denwa
to dial a number	電話番号をダイアルする	denwa bangō wo daiaru suru
Hello!	もしもし	moshimoshi
to ask (vt)	問う	tō
to answer (vi, vt)	出る	deru
to hear (vt)	聞く	kiku
well (adv)	良く	yoku
not well (adv)	良くない	yoku nai
noises (interference)	電波障害	denpa shōgai
receiver	受話器	juwaki
to pick up (~ the phone)	電話に出る	denwa ni deru
to hang up (~ the phone)	電話を切る	denwa wo kiru
busy (adj)	話し中	hanashi chū
to ring (ab. phone)	鳴る	naru
telephone book	電話帳	denwa chō
local (adj)	市内の	shinai no
local call	市内電話	shinai denwa
long distance (~ call)	市外の	shigai no
long-distance call	市外電話	shigai denwa
international (adj)	国際の	kokusai no
international call	国際電話	kokusai denwa

45. Mobile telephone

mobile phone	携帯電話	keitai denwa
display	ディスプレイ	disupurei
button	ボタン	botan
SIM card	SIMカード	shimu kādo
battery	電池	denchi
to be dead (battery)	切れる	kireru
charger	充電器	jūden ki
menu	メニュー	menyū
settings	設定	settei
tune (melody)	メロディー	merodī

to select (vt)	選択する	sentaku suru
calculator	電卓	dentaku
voice mail	ボイスメール	boisu mēru
alarm clock	目覚まし	mezamashi
contacts	連絡先	renraku saki
SMS (text message)	テキストメッセージ	tekisuto messēji
subscriber	加入者	kanyū sha

46. Stationery

ballpoint pen	ボールペン	bōrupen
fountain pen	万年筆	mannenhitsu
pencil	鉛筆	enpitsu
highlighter	蛍光ペン	keikō pen
felt-tip pen	フェルトペン	feruto pen
notepad	メモ帳	memo chō
agenda (diary)	手帳	techō
ruler	定規	jōgi
calculator	電卓	dentaku
eraser	消しゴム	keshigomu
thumbtack	画鋲	gabyō
paper clip	ゼムクリップ	zemu kurippu
glue	糊	nori
stapler	ホッチキス	hocchikisu
hole punch	パンチ	panchi
pencil sharpener	鉛筆削り	enpitsu kezuri

47. Foreign languages

language	言語	gengo
foreign (adj)	外国の	gaikoku no
foreign language	外国語	gaikoku go
to study (vt)	勉強する	benkyō suru
to learn (language, etc.)	学ぶ	manabu
to read (vi, vt)	読む	yomu
to speak (vi, vt)	話す	hanasu
to understand (vt)	理解する	rikai suru
to write (vt)	書く	kaku
fast (adv)	速く	hayaku
slowly (adv)	ゆっくり	yukkuri
fluently (adv)	流ちょうに	ryūchō ni

rules	規則	kisoku
grammar	文法	bunpō
vocabulary	語彙	goi
phonetics	音声学	onseigaku
textbook	教科書	kyōkasho
dictionary	辞書	jisho
teach-yourself book	独習書	dokushū sho
phrasebook	慣用表現集	kanyō hyōgen shū
cassette	カセットテープ	kasettotēpu
videotape	ビデオテープ	bideotēpu
CD, compact disc	CD（シーディー）	shīdī
DVD	DVD［ディーブイディー］	dībuidī
alphabet	アルファベット	arufabetto
to spell (vt)	スペリングを言う	superingu wo iu
pronunciation	発音	hatsuon
accent	なまり［訛り］	namari
with an accent	訛りのある	namari no aru
without an accent	訛りのない	namari no nai
word	単語	tango
meaning	意味	imi
course (e.g., a French ~)	講座	kōza
to sign up	申し込む	mōshikomu
teacher	先生	sensei
translation (process)	翻訳	honyaku
translation (text, etc.)	訳文	yakubun
translator	翻訳者	honyaku sha
interpreter	通訳者	tsūyaku sha
polyglot	ポリグロット	porigurotto
memory	記憶	kioku

MEALS. RESTAURANT

48. Table setting

spoon	スプーン	supūn
knife	ナイフ	naifu
fork	フォーク	fōku
cup (of coffee)	カップ	kappu
plate (dinner ~)	皿	sara
saucer	ソーサー	sōsā
napkin (on table)	ナフキン	nafukin
toothpick	つまようじ ［爪楊枝］	tsumayōji

49. Restaurant

restaurant	レストラン	resutoran
coffee house	喫茶店	kissaten
pub, bar	パブ、バー	pabu, bā
tearoom	喫茶店	kissaten
waiter	ウェイター	weitā
waitress	ウェートレス	wētoresu
bartender	バーテンダー	bātendā
menu	メニュー	menyū
wine list	ワインリスト	wain risuto
to book a table	テーブルを予約する	tēburu wo yoyaku suru
course, dish	料理	ryōri
to order (meal)	注文する	chūmon suru
to make an order	注文する	chūmon suru
aperitif	アペリティフ	aperitifu
appetizer	前菜	zensai
dessert	デザート	dezāto
check	お勘定	okanjō
to pay the check	勘定を払う	kanjō wo harau
to give change	釣り銭を渡す	tsurisen wo watasu
tip	チップ	chippu

50. Meals

food	食べ物	tabemono
to eat (vi, vt)	食べる	taberu
breakfast	朝食	chōshoku
to have breakfast	朝食をとる	chōshoku wo toru
lunch	昼食	chūshoku
to have lunch	昼食をとる	chūshoku wo toru
dinner	夕食	yūshoku
to have dinner	夕食をとる	yūshoku wo toru
appetite	食欲	shokuyoku
Enjoy your meal!	どうぞお召し上がり下さい！	dōzo o meshiagarikudasai!
to open (~ a bottle)	開ける	akeru
to spill (liquid)	こぼす	kobosu
to spill out (vi)	こぼれる	koboreru
to boil (vi)	沸く	waku
to boil (vt)	沸かす	wakasu
boiled (~ water)	沸騰させた	futtō sase ta
to chill, cool down (vt)	冷やす	hiyasu
to chill (vi)	冷える	hieru
taste, flavor	味	aji
aftertaste	後味	atoaji
to be on a diet	ダイエットをする	daietto wo suru
diet	ダイエット	daietto
vitamin	ビタミン	bitamin
calorie	カロリー	karorī
vegetarian (n)	ベジタリアン	bejitarian
vegetarian (adj)	ベジタリアン用の	bejitarian yōno
fats (nutrient)	脂肪	shibō
proteins	タンパク質 [蛋白質]	tanpaku shitsu
carbohydrates	炭水化物	tansuikabutsu
slice (of lemon, ham)	スライス	suraisu
piece (of cake, pie)	一切れ	ichi kire
crumb (of bread)	くず	kuzu

51. Cooked dishes

course, dish	料理	ryōri
cuisine	料理	ryōri
recipe	レシピ	reshipi
portion	一人前	ichi ninmae

| salad | サラダ | sarada |
| soup | スープ | sūpu |

clear soup (broth)	ブイヨン	buiyon
sandwich (bread)	サンドイッチ	sandoicchi
fried eggs	目玉焼き	medamayaki

cutlet (croquette)	クロケット	kuroketto
hamburger (beefburger)	ハンバーガー	hanbāgā
beefsteak	ビーフステーキ	bīfusutēki
stew	シチュー	shichū

side dish	付け合わせ	tsukeawase
spaghetti	スパゲッティ	supagetti
mashed potatoes	マッシュポテト	masshupoteto
pizza	ピザ	piza
porridge (oatmeal, etc.)	ポリッジ	porijji
omelet	オムレツ	omuretsu

boiled (e.g., ~ beef)	煮た	ni ta
smoked (adj)	薫製の	kunsei no
fried (adj)	揚げた	age ta
dried (adj)	干した	hoshi ta
frozen (adj)	冷凍の	reitō no
pickled (adj)	酢漬けの	suzuke no

sweet (sugary)	甘い	amai
salty (adj)	塩味の	shioaji no
cold (adj)	冷たい	tsumetai
hot (adj)	熱い	atsui
bitter (adj)	苦い	nigai
tasty (adj)	美味しい	oishī

to cook in boiling water	水で煮る	mizu de niru
to cook (dinner)	料理をする	ryōri wo suru
to fry (vt)	揚げる	ageru
to heat up (food)	温める	atatameru

to salt (vt)	塩をかける	shio wo kakeru
to pepper (vt)	コショウをかける	koshō wo kakeru
to grate (vt)	すりおろす	suri orosu
peel (n)	皮	kawa
to peel (vt)	皮をむく	kawa wo muku

52. Food

meat	肉	niku
chicken	鶏	niwatori
young chicken	若鶏	wakadori
duck	ダック	dakku

goose	ガチョウ	gachō
game	獲物	emono
turkey	七面鳥	shichimenchuō

pork	豚肉	buta niku
veal	子牛肉	kōshi niku
lamb	子羊肉	kohitsuji niku
beef	牛肉	gyū niku
rabbit	兎肉	usagi niku

sausage (salami, etc.)	ソーセージ	sōsēji
vienna sausage	ソーセージ	sōsēji
bacon	ベーコン	bĕkon
ham	ハム	hamu
gammon (ham)	ガモン	gamon

pâté	パテ	pate
liver	レバー	rebā
lard	ラード	rādo
ground beef	挽肉	hikiniku
tongue	タン	tan

egg	卵	tamago
eggs	卵	tamago
egg white	卵の白身	tamago no shiromi
egg yolk	卵の黄身	tamago no kimi

fish	魚	sakana
seafood	魚介	gyokai
caviar	キャビア	kyabia

crab	カニ［蟹］	kani
shrimp	エビ	ebi
oyster	カキ［牡蠣］	kaki
spiny lobster	伊勢エビ	ise ebi
octopus	タコ	tako
squid	イカ	ika

sturgeon	チョウザメ	chōzame
salmon	サケ［鮭］	sake
halibut	ハリバット	haribatto

cod	タラ［鱈］	tara
mackerel	サバ［鯖］	saba
tuna	マグロ［鮪］	maguro
eel	ウナギ［鰻］	unagi

trout	マス［鱒］	masu
sardine	イワシ	iwashi
pike	カワカマス	kawakamasu
herring	ニシン	nishin
bread	パン	pan

cheese	チーズ	chīzu
sugar	砂糖	satō
salt	塩	shio
rice	米	kome
pasta	パスタ	pasuta
noodles	麺	men
butter	バター	batā
vegetable oil	植物油	shokubutsu yu
sunflower oil	ひまわり油	himawari yu
margarine	マーガリン	māgarin
olives	オリーブ	orību
olive oil	オリーブ油	orību yu
milk	乳、ミルク	nyū, miruku
condensed milk	練乳	rennyū
yogurt	ヨーグルト	yōguruto
sour cream	サワークリーム	sawā kurīmu
cream (of milk)	クリーム	kurīmu
mayonnaise	マヨネーズ	mayonēzu
buttercream	バタークリーム	batā kurīmu
cereal grain (wheat, etc.)	穀物	kokumotsu
flour	小麦粉	komugiko
canned food	缶詰	kanzume
cornflakes	コーンフレーク	kōn furēku
honey	蜂蜜	hachimitsu
jam	ジャム	jamu
chewing gum	チューインガム	chūin gamu

53. Drinks

water	水	mizu
drinking water	飲用水	inyō sui
mineral water	ミネラルウォーター	mineraru wōtā
still (adj)	無炭酸の	mu tansan no
carbonated (adj)	炭酸の	tansan no
sparkling (adj)	発泡性の	happō sei no
ice	水	kōri
with ice	水入りの	kōri iri no
non-alcoholic (adj)	ノンアルコールの	non arukōru no
soft drink	炭酸飲料	tansan inryō
cool soft drink	清涼飲料水	seiryōinryōsui
lemonade	レモネード	remonēdo

liquor	アルコール	arukōru
wine	ワイン	wain
white wine	白ワイン	shiro wain
red wine	赤ワイン	aka wain

liqueur	リキュール	rikyūru
champagne	シャンパン	shanpan
vermouth	ベルモット	berumotto

whisky	ウイスキー	uisukī
vodka	ウォッカ	wokka
gin	ジン	jin
cognac	コニャック	konyakku
rum	ラム酒	ramu shu

coffee	コーヒー	kōhī
black coffee	ブラックコーヒー	burakku kōhī
coffee with milk	ミルク入りコーヒー	miruku iri kōhī
cappuccino	カプチーノ	kapuchīno
instant coffee	インスタントコーヒー	insutanto kōhī

milk	乳, ミルク	nyū, miruku
cocktail	カクテル	kakuteru
milk shake	ミルクセーキ	miruku sēki

juice	ジュース	jūsu
tomato juice	トマトジュース	tomato jūsu
orange juice	オレンジジュース	orenji jūsu
freshly squeezed juice	搾りたてのジュース	shibori tate no jūsu

beer	ビール	bīru
light beer	ライトビール	raito bīru
dark beer	黒ビール	kuro bīru

tea	茶	cha
black tea	紅茶	kō cha
green tea	緑茶	ryoku cha

54. Vegetables

| vegetables | 野菜 | yasai |
| greens | 青物 | aomono |

tomato	トマト	tomato
cucumber	きゅうり [胡瓜]	kyūri
carrot	ニンジン [人参]	ninjin
potato	ジャガイモ	jagaimo
onion	たまねぎ [玉葱]	tamanegi
garlic	ニンニク	ninniku
cabbage	キャベツ	kyabetsu

cauliflower	カリフラワー	karifurawā
Brussels sprouts	メキャベツ	mekyabetsu
broccoli	ブロッコリー	burokkorī
beetroot	テーブルビート	tēburu bīto
eggplant	ナス	nasu
zucchini	ズッキーニ	zukkīni
pumpkin	カボチャ	kabocha
turnip	カブ	kabu
parsley	パセリ	paseri
dill	ディル	diru
lettuce	レタス	retasu
celery	セロリ	serori
asparagus	アスパラガス	asuparagasu
spinach	ホウレンソウ	hōrensō
pea	エンドウ	endō
beans	豆類	mamerui
corn (maize)	トウモロコシ	tōmorokoshi
kidney bean	金時豆	kintoki mame
pepper	コショウ	koshō
radish	ハツカダイコン	hatsukadaikon
artichoke	アーティチョーク	ātichōku

55. Fruits. Nuts

fruit	果物	kudamono
apple	リンゴ	ringo
pear	洋梨	yōnashi
lemon	レモン	remon
orange	オレンジ	orenji
strawberry	イチゴ（苺）	ichigo
mandarin	マンダリン	mandarin
plum	プラム	puramu
peach	モモ［桃］	momo
apricot	アンズ［杏子］	anzu
raspberry	ラズベリー（木苺）	razuberī
pineapple	パイナップル	painappuru
banana	バナナ	banana
watermelon	スイカ	suika
grape	ブドウ［葡萄］	budō
cherry	チェリー	cherī
sour cherry	サワー チェリー	sawā cherī
sweet cherry	スイート チェリー	suīto cherī
melon	メロン	meron
grapefruit	グレープフルーツ	gurēbu furūtsu

avocado	アボカド	abokado
papaya	パパイヤ	papaiya
mango	マンゴー	mangō
pomegranate	ザクロ	zakuro

redcurrant	フサスグリ	fusa suguri
blackcurrant	クロスグリ	kuro suguri
gooseberry	セイヨウスグリ	seiyō suguri
bilberry	ビルベリー	biruberī
blackberry	ブラックベリー	burakku berī

raisin	レーズン	rēzun
fig	イチジク	ichijiku
date	デーツ	dētsu

peanut	ピーナッツ	pīnattsu
almond	アーモンド	āmondo
walnut	クルミ（胡桃）	kurumi
hazelnut	ヘーゼルナッツ	hēzeru nattsu
coconut	ココナッツ	koko nattsu
pistachios	ピスタチオ	pisutachio

56. Bread. Candy

confectionery (pastry)	菓子類	kashi rui
bread	パン	pan
cookies	クッキー	kukkī

chocolate (n)	チョコレート	chokorēto
chocolate (as adj)	チョコレートの	chokorēto no
candy	キャンディー	kyandī
cake (e.g., cupcake)	ケーキ	kēki
cake (e.g., birthday ~)	ケーキ	kēki

| pie (e.g., apple ~) | パイ | pai |
| filling (for cake, pie) | フィリング | firingu |

whole fruit jam	ジャム	jamu
marmalade	マーマレード	māmarēdo
waffle	ワッフル	waffuru
ice-cream	アイスクリーム	aisukurīmu
pudding	プディング	pudingu

57. Spices

salt	塩	shio
salty (adj)	塩味の	shioaji no
to salt (vt)	塩をかける	shio wo kakeru

black pepper	黒コショウ	kuro koshō
red pepper	赤唐辛子	aka tōgarashi
mustard	マスタード	masutādo
horseradish	セイヨウワサビ	seiyō wasabi
condiment	調味料	chōmiryō
spice	香辛料	kōshinryō
sauce	ソース	sōsu
vinegar	酢、ビネガー	su, binegā
anise	アニス	anisu
basil	バジル	bajiru
cloves	クローブ	kurōbu
ginger	生姜、ジンジャー	shōga, jinjā
coriander	コリアンダー	koriandā
cinnamon	シナモン	shinamon
sesame	ゴマ［胡麻］	goma
bay leaf	ローリエ	rōrie
paprika	パプリカ	papurika
caraway	キャラウェイ	kyarawei
saffron	サフラン	safuran

PERSONAL INFORMATION. FAMILY

58. Personal information. Forms

name, first name	名前	namae
family name	姓	sei
date of birth	誕生日	tanjō bi
place of birth	出生地	shusseichi
nationality	国籍	kokuseki
place of residence	住所	jūsho
country	国	kuni
profession (occupation)	職業	shokugyō
gender, sex	性	sei
height	身長	shinchō
weight	体重	taijū

59. Family members. Relatives

mother	母親	hahaoya
father	父親	chichioya
son	息子	musuko
daughter	娘	musume
younger daughter	下の娘	shitano musume
younger son	下の息子	shitano musuko
eldest daughter	長女	chōjo
eldest son	長男	chōnan
brother	兄、弟、兄弟	ani, otōto, kyoōdai
elder brother	兄	ani
younger brother	弟	otōto
sister	姉、妹、姉妹	ane, imōto, shimai
elder sister	姉	ane
younger sister	妹	imōto
cousin (masc.)	従兄弟	itoko
cousin (fem.)	従姉妹	itoko
mom	お母さん	okāsan
dad, daddy	お父さん	otōsan
parents	親	oya
child	子供	kodomo
children	子供	kodomo

grandmother	祖母	sobo
grandfather	祖父	sofu
grandson	孫息子	mago musuko
granddaughter	孫娘	mago musume
grandchildren	孫	mago

uncle	伯父	oji
aunt	伯母	oba
nephew	甥	oi
niece	姪	mei

mother-in-law (wife's mother)	妻の母親	tsuma no hahaoya
father-in-law (husband's father)	義父	gifu
son-in-law (daughter's husband)	娘の夫	musume no otto
stepmother	継母	keibo
stepfather	継父	keifu

infant	乳児	nyūji
baby (infant)	赤ん坊	akanbō
little boy, kid	子供	kodomo

wife	妻	tsuma
husband	夫	otto
spouse (husband)	配偶者	haigū sha
spouse (wife)	配偶者	haigū sha

married (masc.)	既婚の	kikon no
married (fem.)	既婚の	kikon no
single (unmarried)	独身の	dokushin no
bachelor	独身男性	dokushin dansei
divorced (masc.)	離婚した	rikon shi ta
widow	未亡人	mibōjin
widower	男やもめ	otokoyamome

relative	親戚	shinseki
close relative	近い親戚	chikai shinseki
distant relative	遠い親戚	tōi shinseki
relatives	親族	shinzoku
orphan (boy or girl)	孤児	koji
guardian (of minor)	後見人	kōkennin
to adopt (a boy)	養子にする	yōshi ni suru
to adopt (a girl)	養女にする	yōjo ni suru

60. Friends. Coworkers

| friend (masc.) | 友達 | tomodachi |
| friend (fem.) | 友達 | tomodachi |

friendship	友情	yūjō
to be friends	友達だ	tomodachi da
buddy (masc.)	友達	tomodachi
buddy (fem.)	女友達	onna tomodachi
partner	パートナー	pātonā
chief (boss)	長	chō
superior	上司、上役	jōshi, uwayaku
owner, proprietor	経営者	keieisha
subordinate	部下	buka
colleague	同僚	dōryō
acquaintance (person)	知り合い	shiriai
fellow traveler	同調者	dōchō sha
classmate	クラスメート	kurasumēto
neighbor (masc.)	隣人、近所	rinjin, kinjo
neighbor (fem.)	隣人、近所	rinjin, kinjo
neighbors	隣人	rinjin

HUMAN BODY. MEDICINE

61. Head

head	頭	atama
face	顔	kao
nose	鼻	hana
mouth	口	kuchi
eye	眼	me
eyes	両眼	ryōgan
pupil	瞳	hitomi
eyebrow	眉	mayu
eyelash	まつげ	matsuge
eyelid	まぶた	mabuta
tongue	舌	shita
tooth	歯	ha
lips	唇	kuchibiru
cheekbones	頬骨	hōbone
gum	歯茎	haguki
palate	口蓋	kōgai
nostrils	鼻孔	bikō
chin	あご（頤）	ago
jaw	顎	ago
cheek	頬	hō
forehead	額	hitai
temple	こめかみ	komekami
ear	耳	mimi
back of the head	後頭部	kōtōbu
neck	首	kubi
throat	喉	nodo
hair	髪の毛	kaminoke
hairstyle	髪形	kamigata
haircut	髪型	kamigata
wig	かつら	katsura
mustache	口ひげ	kuchihige
beard	あごひげ	agohige
to have (a beard, etc.)	生やしている	hayashi te iru
braid	三つ編み	mitsu ami
sideburns	もみあげ	momiage
red-haired (adj)	赤毛の	akage no

gray (hair)	白髪の	hakuhatsu no
bald (adj)	はげ頭の	hageatama no
bald patch	はげた部分	hage ta bubun
ponytail	ポニーテール	ponītēru
bangs	前髪	maegami

62. Human body

hand	手	te
arm	腕	ude
finger	指	yubi
toe	つま先	tsumasaki
thumb	親指	oyayubi
little finger	小指	koyubi
nail	爪	tsume
fist	拳	kobushi
palm	手のひら	tenohira
wrist	手首	tekubi
forearm	前腕	zen wan
elbow	肘	hiji
shoulder	肩	kata
leg	足 [脚]	ashi
foot	足	ashi
knee	膝	hiza
calf (part of leg)	ふくらはぎ	fuku ra hagi
hip	腰	koshi
heel	かかと [踵]	kakato
body	身体	shintai
stomach	腹	hara
chest	胸	mune
breast	乳房	chibusa
flank	脇腹	wakibara
back	背中	senaka
lower back	腰背部	yōwa ibu
waist	腰	koshi
navel	へそ [臍]	heso
buttocks	臀部	denbu
bottom	尻	shiri
beauty mark	美人ぼくろ	bijinbokuro
birthmark	母斑	bohan
tattoo	タトゥー	tatū
scar	傷跡	kizuato

63. Diseases

sickness	病気	byōki
to be sick	病気になる	byōki ni naru
health	健康	kenkō
runny nose (coryza)	鼻水	hanamizu
angina	狭心症	kyōshinshō
cold (illness)	風邪	kaze
to catch a cold	風邪をひく	kaze wo hiku
bronchitis	気管支炎	kikanshien
pneumonia	肺炎	haien
flu, influenza	インフルエンザ	infuruenza
near-sighted (adj)	近視の	kinshi no
far-sighted (adj)	遠視の	enshi no
strabismus (crossed eyes)	斜視	shashi
cross-eyed (adj)	斜視の	shashi no
cataract	白内障	hakunaishō
glaucoma	緑内障	ryokunaishō
stroke	脳卒中	nōsocchū
heart attack	心臓発作	shinzō hossa
myocardial infarction	心筋梗塞	shinkinkōsoku
paralysis	まひ [麻痺]	mahi
to paralyze (vt)	まひさせる	mahi saseru
allergy	アレルギー	arerugī
asthma	ぜんそく [喘息]	zensoku
diabetes	糖尿病	tōnyō byō
toothache	歯痛	shitsū
caries	カリエス	kariesu
diarrhea	下痢	geri
constipation	便秘	benpi
stomach upset	胃のむかつき	i no mukatsuki
food poisoning	食中毒	shokuchūdoku
to have a food poisoning	食中毒にかかる	shokuchūdoku ni kakaru
arthritis	関節炎	kansetsu en
rickets	くる病	kuru yamai
rheumatism	リューマチ	ryūmachi
atherosclerosis	アテローム性動脈硬化	ate rōmu sei dōmyaku kōka
gastritis	胃炎	ien
appendicitis	虫垂炎	chūsuien
cholecystitis	胆嚢炎	tannō en
ulcer	潰瘍	kaiyō

measles	麻疹	hashika
German measles	風疹	fūshin
jaundice	黄疸	ōdan
hepatitis	肝炎	kanen
schizophrenia	統合失調症	tōgō shicchō shō
rabies (hydrophobia)	恐水病	kyōsuibyō
neurosis	神経症	shinkeishō
concussion	脳震とう（脳震盪）	nōshintō
cancer	がん [癌]	gan
sclerosis	硬化症	kōka shō
multiple sclerosis	多発性硬化症	tahatsu sei kōka shō
alcoholism	アルコール依存症	arukōru izon shō
alcoholic (n)	アルコール依存症患者	arukōru izon shō kanja
syphilis	梅毒	baidoku
AIDS	エイズ	eizu
tumor	腫瘍	shuyō
malignant (adj)	悪性の	akusei no
benign (adj)	良性の	ryōsei no
fever	発熱	hatsunetsu
malaria	マラリア	mararia
gangrene	壊疽	eso
seasickness	船酔い	fune yoi
epilepsy	てんかん [癲癇]	tenkan
epidemic	伝染病	densen byō
typhus	チフス	chifusu
tuberculosis	結核	kekkaku
cholera	コレラ	korera
plague (bubonic ~)	ペスト	pesuto

64. Symptoms. Treatments. Part 1

symptom	兆候	chōkō
temperature	体温	taion
high temperature	熱	netsu
pulse	脈拍	myakuhaku
giddiness	目まい [眩暈]	memai
hot (adj)	熱い	atsui
shivering	震え	furue
pale (e.g., ~ face)	青白い	aojiroi
cough	咳	seki
to cough (vi)	咳をする	seki wo suru
to sneeze (vi)	くしゃみをする	kushami wo suru

faint	気絶	kizetsu
to faint (vi)	気絶する	kizetsu suru
bruise (hématome)	打ち身	uchimi
bump (lump)	たんこぶ	tankobu
to bruise oneself	あざができる	aza ga dekiru
bruise (contusion)	打撲傷	dabokushō
to get bruised	打撲する	daboku suru
to limp (vi)	足を引きずる	ashi wo hikizuru
dislocation	脱臼	dakkyū
to dislocate (vt)	脱臼する	dakkyū suru
fracture	骨折	kossetsu
to have a fracture	骨折する	kossetsu suru
cut (e.g., paper ~)	切り傷	kirikizu
to cut oneself	切り傷を負う	kirikizu wo ō
bleeding	出血	shukketsu
burn (injury)	火傷	yakedo
to scald oneself	火傷する	yakedo suru
to prick (vt)	刺す	sasu
to prick oneself	自分を刺す	jibun wo sasu
to injure (vt)	けがする	kega suru
injury	けが［怪我］	kega
wound	負傷	fushō
trauma	外傷	gaishō
to be delirious	熱に浮かされる	netsu ni ukasareru
to stutter (vi)	どもる	domoru
sunstroke	日射病	nisshabyō

65. Symptoms. Treatments. Part 2

pain	痛み	itami
splinter (in foot, etc.)	とげ［棘］	toge
sweat (perspiration)	汗	ase
to sweat (perspire)	汗をかく	ase wo kaku
vomiting	嘔吐	ōto
convulsions	けいれん［痙攣］	keiren
pregnant (adj)	妊娠している	ninshin shi te iru
to be born	生まれる	umareru
delivery, labor	分娩	bumben
to deliver (~ a baby)	分娩する	bumben suru
abortion	妊娠中絶	ninshin chūzetsu
breathing, respiration	呼吸	kokyū
inhalation	息を吸うこと	iki wo sū koto

exhalation	息を吐くこと	iki wo haku koto
to exhale (vi)	息を吐く	iki wo haku
to inhale (vi)	息を吸う	iki wo sū
disabled person	障害者	shōgai sha
cripple	身障者	shinshōsha
drug addict	麻薬中毒者	mayaku chūdoku sha
deaf (adj)	ろうの［聾の］	rō no
dumb, mute	口のきけない	kuchi no kike nai
deaf-and-dumb (adj)	ろうあの［聾唖の］	rōa no
mad, insane (adj)	狂気の	kyōki no
madman	狂人	kyōjin
madwoman	狂女	kyōjo
to go insane	気が狂う	ki ga kurū
gene	遺伝子	idenshi
immunity	免疫	meneki
hereditary (adj)	遺伝性の	iden sei no
congenital (adj)	先天性の	senten sei no
virus	ウィルス	wirusu
microbe	細菌	saikin
bacterium	バクテリア	bakuteria
infection	伝染	densen

66. Symptoms. Treatments. Part 3

hospital	病院	byōin
patient	患者	kanja
diagnosis	診断	shindan
cure	療養	ryōyō
medical treatment	治療	chiryō
to get treatment	治療を受ける	chiryō wo ukeru
to treat (vt)	治療する	chiryō suru
to nurse (look after)	看護する	kango suru
care (nursing ~)	看護	kango
operation, surgery	手術	shujutsu
to bandage (head, limb)	包帯をする	hōtai wo suru
bandaging	包帯を巻くこと	hōtai wo maku koto
vaccination	予防接種	yobō sesshu
to vaccinate (vt)	予防接種をする	yobō sesshu wo suru
injection, shot	注射	chūsha
to give an injection	注射する	chūsha suru
attack	発作	hossa
amputation	切断手術	setsudan shujutsu

to amputate (vt)	切断する	setsudan suru
coma	昏睡	konsui
to be in a coma	昏睡状態になる	konsui jōtai ni naru
intensive care	集中治療	shūchū chiryō
to recover (~ from flu)	回復する	kaifuku suru
state (patient's ~)	体調	taichō
consciousness	意識	ishiki
memory (faculty)	記憶	kioku
to extract (tooth)	抜く	nuku
filling	詰め物	tsume mono
to fill (a tooth)	詰め物をする	tsume mono wo suru
hypnosis	催眠術	saimin jutsu
to hypnotize (vt)	催眠術をかける	saimin jutsu wo kakeru

67. Medicine. Drugs. Accessories

medicine, drug	薬	kusuri
remedy	治療薬	chiryō yaku
to prescribe (vt)	処方する	shohō suru
prescription	処方	shohō
tablet, pill	錠剤	jōzai
ointment	軟膏	nankō
ampule	アンプル	anpuru
mixture	調合薬	chōgō yaku
syrup	シロップ	shiroppu
pill	丸剤	gan zai
powder	粉薬	konagusuri
bandage	包帯	hōtai
cotton wool	脱脂綿	dasshimen
iodine	ヨード	yōdo
Band-Aid	ばんそうこう [絆創膏]	bansōkō
eyedropper	アイドロッパー	aidoroppā
thermometer	体温計	taionkei
syringe	注射器	chūsha ki
wheelchair	車椅子	kurumaisu
crutches	松葉杖	matsubazue
painkiller	痛み止め	itami tome
laxative	下剤	gezai
spirit (ethanol)	エタノール	etanoru
medicinal herbs	薬草	yakusō
herbal (~ tea)	薬草の	yakusō no

APARTMENT

68. Apartment

apartment	アパート	apāto
room	部屋	heya
bedroom	寝室	shinshitsu
dining room	食堂	shokudō
living room	居間	ima
study (home office)	書斎	shosai
entry room	玄関	genkan
bathroom	浴室	yokushitsu
half bath	トイレ	toire
ceiling	天井	tenjō
floor	床	yuka
corner	隅	sumi

69. Furniture. Interior

furniture	家具	kagu
table	テーブル	tēburu
chair	椅子	isu
bed	ベッド	beddo
couch, sofa	ソファ	sofa
armchair	肘掛け椅子	hijikake isu
bookcase	書棚	shodana
shelf	棚	tana
set of shelves	違い棚	chigaidana
wardrobe	ワードローブ	wādo rōbu
coat rack	ウォールハンガー	wōru hangā
coat stand	コートスタンド	kōto sutando
dresser	チェスト	chesuto
coffee table	コーヒーテーブル	kōhī tēburu
mirror	鏡	kagami
carpet	カーペット	kāpetto
rug, small carpet	マット	matto
fireplace	暖炉	danro
candle	ろうそく	rōsoku

candlestick	ろうそく立て	rōsoku date
drapes	カーテン	kāten
wallpaper	壁紙	kabegami
blinds (jalousie)	ブラインド	buraindo

table lamp	テーブルランプ	tēburu ranpu
wall lamp (sconce)	ウォールランプ	wōru ranpu
floor lamp	フロアスタンド	furoa sutando
chandelier	シャンデリア	shanderia

leg (of chair, table)	脚	ashi
armrest	肘掛け	hijikake
back (backrest)	背もたれ	semotare
drawer	引き出し	hikidashi

70. Bedding

bedclothes	寝具	shingu
pillow	枕	makura
pillowcase	枕カバー	makura kabā
blanket (comforter)	毛布	mōfu
sheet	シーツ	shītsu
bedspread	ベッドカバー	beddo kabā

71. Kitchen

kitchen	台所	daidokoro
gas	ガス	gasu
gas cooker	ガスコンロ	gasu konro
electric cooker	電気コンロ	denki konro
oven	オーブン	ōbun
microwave oven	電子レンジ	denshi renji

refrigerator	冷蔵庫	reizōko
freezer	冷凍庫	reitōko
dishwasher	食器洗い機	shokkiarai ki

meat grinder	肉挽き器	niku hiki ki
juicer	ジューサー	jūsā
toaster	トースター	tōsutā
mixer	ハンドミキサー	hando mikisā

coffee maker	コーヒーメーカー	kōhī mēkā
coffee pot	コーヒーポット	kōhī potto
coffee grinder	コーヒーグラインダー	kōhī guraindā

| kettle | やかん | yakan |
| teapot | 急須 | kyūsu |

lid	蓋 ［ふた］	futa
tea strainer	茶漉し	chakoshi
spoon	さじ ［匙］	saji
teaspoon	茶さじ	cha saji
tablespoon	大さじ ［大匙］	ōsaji
fork	フォーク	fōku
knife	ナイフ	naifu
tableware (dishes)	食器	shokki
plate (dinner ~)	皿	sara
saucer	ソーサー	sōsā
shot glass	ショットグラス	shotto gurasu
glass (~ of water)	コップ	koppu
cup	カップ	kappu
sugar bowl	砂糖入れ	satō ire
salt shaker	塩入れ	shio ire
pepper shaker	胡椒入れ	koshō ire
butter dish	バター皿	batā zara
saucepan	両手鍋	ryō tenabe
frying pan	フライパン	furaipan
ladle	おたま	o tama
colander	水切りボール	mizukiri bōru
tray	配膳盆	haizen bon
bottle	ボトル	botoru
jar (glass)	ジャー、瓶	jā, bin
can	缶	kan
bottle opener	栓抜き	sen nuki
can opener	缶切り	kankiri
corkscrew	コルク抜き	koruku nuki
filter	フィルター	firutā
to filter (vt)	フィルターにかける	firutā ni kakeru
trash	ゴミ ［ごみ］	gomi
trash can	ゴミ箱	gomibako

72. Bathroom

bathroom	浴室	yokushitsu
water	水	mizu
tap, faucet	蛇口	jaguchi
hot water	温水	onsui
cold water	冷水	reisui
toothpaste	歯磨き粉	hamigakiko
to brush one's teeth	歯を磨く	ha wo migaku

toothbrush	歯ブラシ	haburashi
to shave (vi)	ひげを剃る	hige wo soru
shaving foam	シェービングフォーム	shēbingu fōmu
razor	剃刀	kamisori
to wash (one's hands, etc.)	洗う	arau
to take a bath	風呂に入る	furo ni hairu
shower	シャワー	shawā
to take a shower	シャワーを浴びる	shawā wo abiru
bathtub	浴槽	yokusō
toilet (toilet bowl)	トイレ、便器	toire, benki
sink (washbasin)	洗面台	senmen dai
soap	石鹸	sekken
soap dish	石鹸皿	sekken zara
sponge	スポンジ	suponji
shampoo	シャンプー	shanpū
towel	タオル	taoru
bathrobe	バスローブ	basurōbu
laundry (process)	洗濯	sentaku
washing machine	洗濯機	sentaku ki
to do the laundry	洗濯する	sentaku suru
laundry detergent	洗剤	senzai

73. Household appliances

TV set	テレビ	terebi
tape recorder	テープレコーダー	tēpurekōdā
video, VCR	ビデオ	bideo
radio	ラジオ	rajio
player (CD, MP3, etc.)	プレーヤー	purēyā
video projector	ビデオプロジェクター	bideo purojekutā
home movie theater	ホームシアター	hōmu shiatā
DVD player	DVDプレーヤー	dībuidī purēyā
amplifier	アンプ	anpu
video game console	ゲーム機	gēmu ki
video camera	ビデオカメラ	bideo kamera
camera (photo)	カメラ	kamera
digital camera	デジタルカメラ	dejitaru kamera
vacuum cleaner	掃除機	sōji ki
iron (e.g., steam ~)	アイロン	airon
ironing board	アイロン台	airondai
telephone	電話	denwa
mobile phone	携帯電話	keitai denwa

typewriter	タイプライター	taipuraitā
sewing machine	ミシン	mishin
microphone	マイクロフォン	maikurofon
headphones	ヘッドホン	heddohon
remote control (TV)	リモコン	rimokon
CD, compact disc	CD（シーディー）	shīdī
cassette	カセットテープ	kasettotēpu
vinyl record	レコード	rekōdo

THE EARTH. WEATHER

74. Outer space

cosmos	宇宙	uchū
space (as adj)	宇宙の	uchū no
outer space	宇宙空間	uchū kūkan
world	世界	sekai
universe	宇宙	uchū
galaxy	銀河系	gingakei
star	星	hoshi
constellation	星座	seiza
planet	惑星	wakusei
satellite	衛星	eisei
meteorite	隕石	inseki
comet	彗星	suisei
asteroid	小惑星	shōwakusei
orbit	軌道	kidō
to revolve (~ around the Earth)	公転する	kōten suru
atmosphere	大気	taiki
the Sun	太陽	taiyō
solar system	太陽系	taiyōkei
solar eclipse	日食	nisshoku
the Earth	地球	chikyū
the Moon	月	tsuki
Mars	火星	kasei
Venus	金星	kinsei
Jupiter	木星	mokusei
Saturn	土星	dosei
Mercury	水星	suisei
Uranus	天王星	tennōsei
Neptune	海王星	kaiōsei
Pluto	冥王星	meiōsei
Milky Way	天の川	amanogawa
Great Bear	おおぐま座	ōguma za
North Star	北極星	hokkyokusei
Martian	火星人	kasei jin

extraterrestrial (n)	宇宙人	uchū jin
alien	異星人	i hoshi jin
flying saucer	空飛ぶ円盤	sora tobu enban
spaceship	宇宙船	uchūsen
space station	宇宙ステーション	uchū sutēshon
blast-off	打ち上げ	uchiage
engine	エンジン	enjin
nozzle	ノズル	nozuru
fuel	燃料	nenryō
cockpit, flight deck	コックピット	kokkupitto
antenna	アンテナ	antena
porthole	舷窓	gensō
solar battery	太陽電池	taiyō denchi
spacesuit	宇宙服	uchū fuku
weightlessness	無重力	mu jūryoku
oxygen	酸素	sanso
docking (in space)	ドッキング	dokkingu
to dock (vi, vt)	ドッキングする	dokkingu suru
observatory	天文台	tenmondai
telescope	望遠鏡	bōenkyō
to observe (vt)	観察する	kansatsu suru
to explore (vt)	探索する	tansaku suru

75. The Earth

the Earth	地球	chikyū
globe (the Earth)	世界	sekai
planet	惑星	wakusei
atmosphere	大気	taiki
geography	地理学	chiri gaku
nature	自然	shizen
globe (table ~)	地球儀	chikyūgi
map	地図	chizu
atlas	地図帳	chizu chō
Europe	ヨーロッパ	yōroppa
Asia	アジア	ajia
Africa	アフリカ	afurika
Australia	オーストラリア	ōsutoraria
America	アメリカ	amerika
North America	北アメリカ	kita amerika

South America	南アメリカ	minami amerika
Antarctica	南極大陸	nankyokutairiku
the Arctic	北極	hokkyoku

76. Cardinal directions

north	北	kita
to the north	北へ	kita he
in the north	北に	kita ni
northern (adj)	北の	kita no
south	南	minami
to the south	南へ	minami he
in the south	南に	minami ni
southern (adj)	南の	minami no
west	西	nishi
to the west	西へ	nishi he
in the west	西に	nishi ni
western (adj)	西の	nishi no
east	東	higashi
to the east	東へ	higashi he
in the east	東に	higashi ni
eastern (adj)	東の	higashi no

77. Sea. Ocean

sea	海	umi
ocean	海洋	kaiyō
gulf (bay)	湾	wan
straits	海峡	kaikyō
solid ground	乾燥地	kansō chi
continent (mainland)	大陸	tairiku
island	島	shima
peninsula	半島	hantō
archipelago	多島海	tatōkai
bay, cove	入り江	irie
harbor	泊地	hakuchi
lagoon	潟	kata
cape	岬	misaki
atoll	環礁	kanshō
reef	暗礁	anshō
coral	サンゴ	sango
coral reef	サンゴ礁	sangoshō

deep (adj)	深い	fukai
depth (deep water)	深さ	fuka sa
abyss	深淵	shinen
trench (e.g., Mariana ~)	海溝	kaikō
current, stream	海流	kairyū
to surround (bathe)	取り囲む	torikakomu
shore	海岸	kaigan
coast	沿岸	engan
high tide	満潮	manchō
low tide	干潮	kanchō
sandbank	砂州	sasu
bottom	底	soko
wave	波	nami
crest (~ of a wave)	波頭	namigashira
froth (foam)	泡	awa
storm	嵐	arashi
hurricane	ハリケーン	harikēn
tsunami	津波	tsunami
calm (dead ~)	凪	nagi
quiet, calm (adj)	穏やかな	odayaka na
pole	極地	kyokuchi
polar (adj)	極地の	kyokuchi no
latitude	緯度	ido
longitude	経度	keido
parallel	度線	dosen
equator	赤道	sekidō
sky	空	sora
horizon	地平線	chiheisen
air	空気	kūki
lighthouse	灯台	tōdai
to dive (vi)	飛び込む	tobikomu
to sink (ab. boat)	沈没する	chinbotsu suru
treasures	宝	takara

78. Seas' and Oceans' names

Atlantic Ocean	大西洋	taiseiyō
Indian Ocean	インド洋	indoyō
Pacific Ocean	太平洋	taiheiyō
Arctic Ocean	北氷洋	kitakōriyō
Black Sea	黒海	kokkai

Red Sea	紅海	kōkai
Yellow Sea	黄海	kōkai
White Sea	白海	hakkai

Caspian Sea	カスピ海	kasupikai
Dead Sea	死海	shikai
Mediterranean Sea	地中海	chichūkai

| Aegean Sea | エーゲ海 | ēgekai |
| Adriatic Sea | アドリア海 | adoriakai |

Arabian Sea	アラビア海	arabia kai
Sea of Japan	日本海	nihonkai
Bering Sea	ベーリング海	bēringukai
South China Sea	南シナ海	minami shinakai

Coral Sea	珊瑚海	sangokai
Tasman Sea	タスマン海	tasumankai
Caribbean Sea	カリブ海	karibukai

| Barents Sea | バレンツ海 | barentsukai |
| Kara Sea | カラ海 | karakai |

North Sea	北海	hokkai
Baltic Sea	バルト海	barutokai
Norwegian Sea	ノルウェー海	noruwē umi

79. Mountains

mountain	山	yama
mountain range	山脈	sanmyaku
mountain ridge	山稜	sanryō

summit, top	頂上	chōjō
peak	とがった山頂	togatta sanchō
foot (of mountain)	麓	fumoto
slope (mountainside)	山腹	sanpuku

volcano	火山	kazan
active volcano	活火山	kakkazan
dormant volcano	休火山	kyūkazan

eruption	噴火	funka
crater	噴火口	funkakō
magma	岩漿、マグマ	ganshō, maguma
lava	溶岩	yōgan
molten (~ lava)	溶…	yō …

| canyon | 峡谷 | kyōkoku |
| gorge | 峡谷 | kyōkoku |

| crevice | 裂け目 | sakeme |
| abyss (chasm) | 奈落の底 | naraku no soko |

pass, col	峠	tōge
plateau	高原	kōgen
cliff	断崖	dangai
hill	丘	oka

glacier	氷河	hyōga
waterfall	滝	taki
geyser	間欠泉	kanketsusen
lake	湖	mizūmi

plain	平原	heigen
landscape	風景	fūkei
echo	こだま	kodama

alpinist	登山家	tozan ka
rock climber	ロッククライマー	rokku kuraimā
to conquer (in climbing)	征服する	seifuku suru
climb (an easy ~)	登山	tozan

80. Mountains names

Alps	アルプス山脈	arupusu sanmyaku
Mont Blanc	モンブラン	monburan
Pyrenees	ピレネー山脈	pirenē sanmyaku

Carpathians	カルパティア山脈	karupatia sanmyaku
Ural Mountains	ウラル山脈	uraru sanmyaku
Caucasus	コーカサス山脈	kōkasasu sanmyaku
Elbrus	エルブルス山	eruburusu san

Altai	アルタイ山脈	arutai sanmyaku
Tien Shan	天山山脈	amayama sanmyaku
Pamir Mountains	パミール高原	pamīru kōgen
Himalayas	ヒマラヤ	himaraya
Everest	エベレスト	eberesuto

| Andes | アンデス山脈 | andesu sanmyaku |
| Kilimanjaro | キリマンジャロ | kirimanjaro |

81. Rivers

river	川	kawa
spring (natural source)	泉	izumi
riverbed	川床	kawadoko
basin	流域	ryūiki

to flow into ...	…に流れ込む	… ni nagarekomu
tributary	支流	shiryū
bank (of river)	川岸	kawagishi
current, stream	流れ	nagare
downstream (adv)	下流の	karyū no
upstream (adv)	上流の	jōryū no
inundation	洪水	kōzui
flooding	氾濫	hanran
to overflow (vi)	氾濫する	hanran suru
to flood (vt)	水浸しにする	mizubitashi ni suru
shallows (shoal)	浅瀬	asase
rapids	急流	kyūryū
dam	ダム	damu
canal	運河	unga
artificial lake	ため池 [溜池]	tameike
sluice, lock	水門	suimon
water body (pond, etc.)	水域	suīki
swamp, bog	沼地	numachi
marsh	湿地	shicchi
whirlpool	渦	uzu
stream (brook)	小川	ogawa
drinking (ab. water)	飲用の	inyō no
fresh (~ water)	淡…	tan …
ice	氷	kōri
to freeze (ab. river, etc.)	氷結する	hyōketsu suru

82. Rivers' names

Seine	セーヌ川	sēnu gawa
Loire	ロワール川	rowāru gawa
Thames	テムズ川	temuzu gawa
Rhine	ライン川	rain gawa
Danube	ドナウ川	donau gawa
Volga	ヴォルガ川	voruga gawa
Don	ドン川	don gawa
Lena	レナ川	rena gawa
Yellow River	黄河	kōga
Yangtze	長江	chōkō
Mekong	メコン川	mekon gawa
Ganges	ガンジス川	ganjisu gawa

Nile River	ナイル川	nairu gawa
Congo	コンゴ川	kongo gawa
Okavango	オカヴァンゴ川	okavango gawa
Zambezi	ザンベジ川	zanbeji gawa
Limpopo	リンポポ川	rinpopo gawa
Mississippi River	ミシシッピ川	mishishippi gawa

83. Forest

forest	森林	shinrin
forest (as adj)	森林の	shinrin no
thick forest	密林	mitsurin
grove	木立	kodachi
forest clearing	空き地	akichi
thicket	やぶ ［藪］	yabu
scrubland	低木地域	teiboku chīki
footpath (troddenpath)	小道	komichi
gully	ガリ	gari
tree	木	ki
leaf	葉	ha
leaves	葉っぱ	happa
fall of leaves	落葉	rakuyō
to fall (ab. leaves)	落ちる	ochiru
top (of the tree)	木のてっぺん	kinoteppen
branch	枝	eda
bough	主枝	shushi
bud (on shrub, tree)	芽 ［め］	me
needle (of pine tree)	松葉	matsuba
pine cone	松ぼっくり	matsubokkuri
hollow (in a tree)	樹洞	kihora
nest	巣	su
burrow (animal hole)	巣穴	su ana
trunk	幹	miki
root	根	ne
bark	樹皮	juhi
moss	コケ ［苔］	koke
to uproot (vt)	根こそぎにする	nekosogi ni suru
to chop down	切り倒す	kiritaosu
to deforest (vt)	切り払う	kiriharau
tree stump	切り株	kirikabu
campfire	焚火	takibi

| forest fire | 森林火災 | shinrin kasai |
| to extinguish (vt) | 火を消す | hi wo kesu |

forest ranger	森林警備隊員	shinrin keibi taīn
protection	保護	hogo
to protect (~ nature)	保護する	hogo suru
poacher	密漁者	mitsuryō sha
trap (e.g., bear ~)	罠	wana

to pick (mushrooms)	摘み集める	tsumi atsumeru
to pick (berries)	採る	toru
to lose one's way	道に迷う	michi ni mayō

84. Natural resources

natural resources	天然資源	tennen shigen
minerals	鉱物資源	kōbutsu shigen
deposits	鉱床	kōshō
field (e.g., oilfield)	田	den

to mine (extract)	採掘する	saikutsu suru
mining (extraction)	採掘	saikutsu
ore	鉱石	kōseki
mine (e.g., for coal)	鉱山	kōzan
mine shaft, pit	立坑	tatekō
miner	鉱山労働者	kōzan rōdō sha

| gas | ガス | gasu |
| gas pipeline | ガスパイプライン | gasu paipurain |

oil (petroleum)	石油	sekiyu
oil pipeline	石油パイプライン	sekiyu paipurain
oil well	油井	yusei
derrick	油井やぐら	yusei ya gura
tanker	タンカー	tankā

sand	砂	suna
limestone	石灰岩	sekkaigan
gravel	砂利	jari
peat	泥炭	deitan
clay	粘土	nendo
coal	石炭	sekitan

iron	鉄	tetsu
gold	金	kin
silver	銀	gin
nickel	ニッケル	nikkeru
copper	銅	dō
zinc	亜鉛	aen
manganese	マンガン	mangan

| mercury | 水銀 | suigin |
| lead | 鉛 | namari |

mineral	鉱物	kōbutsu
crystal	水晶	suishō
marble	大理石	dairiseki
uranium	ウラン	uran

85. Weather

weather	天気	tenki
weather forecast	天気予報	tenki yohō
temperature	温度	ondo
thermometer	温度計	ondo kei
barometer	気圧計	kiatsu kei

humid (adj)	湿度の	shitsudo no
humidity	湿度	shitsudo
heat (extreme ~)	猛暑	mōsho
hot (torrid)	暑い	atsui
it's hot	暑いです	atsui desu

| it's warm | 暖かいです | atatakai desu |
| warm (moderately hot) | 暖かい | atatakai |

| it's cold | 寒いです | samui desu |
| cold (adj) | 寒い | samui |

sun	太陽	taiyō
to shine (vi)	照る	teru
sunny (day)	晴れの	hare no
to come up (vi)	昇る	noboru
to set (vi)	沈む	shizumu

cloud	雲	kumo
cloudy (adj)	曇りの	kumori no
rain cloud	雨雲	amagumo
somber (gloomy)	どんよりした	donyori shi ta

rain	雨	ame
it's raining	雨が降っている	ame ga futte iru
rainy (day)	雨の	ame no
to drizzle (vi)	そぼ降る	sobofuru

pouring rain	土砂降りの雨	doshaburi no ame
downpour	大雨	ōame
heavy (e.g., ~ rain)	激しい	hageshī
puddle	水溜り	mizutamari
to get wet (in rain)	ぬれる ［濡れる］	nureru
fog (mist)	霧	kiri

foggy	霧の	kiri no
snow	雪	yuki
it's snowing	雪が降っている	yuki ga futte iru

86. Severe weather. Natural disasters

thunderstorm	雷雨	raiu
lightning (~ strike)	稲妻	inazuma
to flash (vi)	ピカッと光る	pikatto hikaru

thunder	雷	kaminari
to thunder (vi)	雷が鳴る	kaminari ga naru
it's thundering	雷が鳴っている	kaminari ga natte iru

| hail | ひょう [雹] | hyō |
| it's hailing | ひょうが降っている | hyō ga futte iru |

| to flood (vt) | 水浸しにする | mizubitashi ni suru |
| flood, inundation | 洪水 | kōzui |

earthquake	地震	jishin
tremor, quake	震動	shindō
epicenter	震源地	shingen chi

| eruption | 噴火 | funka |
| lava | 溶岩 | yōgan |

twister	旋風	senpū
tornado	竜巻	tatsumaki
typhoon	台風	taifū

hurricane	ハリケーン	harikēn
storm	暴風	bōfū
tsunami	津波	tsunami

cyclone	サイクロン	saikuron
bad weather	悪い天気	warui tenki
fire (accident)	火事	kaji
disaster	災害	saigai
meteorite	隕石	inseki

avalanche	雪崩	nadare
snowslide	雪崩	nadare
blizzard	猛吹雪	mō fubuki
snowstorm	吹雪	fubuki

FAUNA

87. Mammals. Predators

predator	肉食獣	nikushoku juu
tiger	トラ［虎］	tora
lion	ライオン	raion
wolf	オオカミ	ōkami
fox	キツネ［狐］	kitsune
jaguar	ジャガー	jagā
leopard	ヒョウ［豹］	hyō
cheetah	チーター	chītā
black panther	黒豹	kuro hyō
puma	ピューマ	pyūma
snow leopard	雪豹	yuki hyō
lynx	オオヤマネコ	ōyamaneko
coyote	コヨーテ	koyōte
jackal	ジャッカル	jakkaru
hyena	ハイエナ	haiena

88. Wild animals

animal	動物	dōbutsu
beast (animal)	獣	shishi
squirrel	リス	risu
hedgehog	ハリネズミ［針鼠］	harinezumi
hare	ヘア	hea
rabbit	ウサギ［兎］	usagi
badger	アナグマ	anaguma
raccoon	アライグマ	araiguma
hamster	ハムスター	hamusutā
marmot	マーモット	māmotto
mole	モグラ	mogura
mouse	ネズミ	nezumi
rat	ラット	ratto
bat	コウモリ［蝙蝠］	kōmori
ermine	オコジョ	okojo
sable	クロテン	kuroten

marten	マツテン	matsu ten
weasel	イタチ（鼬、鼬鼠）	itachi
mink	ミンク	minku

| beaver | ビーバー | bībā |
| otter | カワウソ | kawauso |

horse	ウマ［馬］	uma
moose	ヘラジカ（箆鹿）	herajika
deer	シカ［鹿］	shika
camel	ラクダ［駱駝］	rakuda

bison	アメリカバイソン	amerika baison
aurochs	ヨーロッパバイソン	yōroppa baison
buffalo	水牛	suigyū

zebra	シマウマ［縞馬］	shimauma
antelope	レイヨウ	reiyō
roe deer	ノロジカ	noro jika
fallow deer	ダマジカ	damajika
chamois	シャモア	shamoa
wild boar	イノシシ［猪］	inoshishi

whale	クジラ［鯨］	kujira
seal	アザラシ	azarashi
walrus	セイウチ［海象］	seiuchi
fur seal	オットセイ［膃肭臍］	ottosei
dolphin	いるか［海豚］	iruka

bear	クマ［熊］	kuma
polar bear	ホッキョクグマ	hokkyokuguma
panda	パンダ	panda

monkey	サル［猿］	saru
chimpanzee	チンパンジー	chinpanjī
orangutan	オランウータン	oranwutan
gorilla	ゴリラ	gorira
macaque	マカク	makaku
gibbon	テナガザル	tenagazaru

elephant	ゾウ［象］	zō
rhinoceros	サイ［犀］	sai
giraffe	キリン	kirin
hippopotamus	カバ［河馬］	kaba

| kangaroo | カンガルー | kangarū |
| koala (bear) | コアラ | koara |

mongoose	マングース	mangūsu
chinchilla	チンチラ	chinchira
skunk	スカンク	sukanku
porcupine	ヤマアラシ	yamārashi

89. Domestic animals

cat	猫	neko
tomcat	オス猫	osu neko
dog	犬	inu
horse	ウマ［馬］	uma
stallion	種馬	taneuma
mare	雌馬	meuma
cow	雌牛	meushi
bull	雄牛	ōshi
ox	去勢牛	kyosei ushi
sheep	羊	hitsuji
ram	雄羊	ohitsuji
goat	ヤギ［山羊］	yagi
billy goat, he-goat	雄ヤギ	oyagi
donkey	ロバ	roba
mule	ラバ	raba
pig	ブタ［豚］	buta
piglet	子豚	kobuta
rabbit	カイウサギ［飼兎］	kai usagi
hen (chicken)	ニワトリ［鶏］	niwatori
rooster	おんどり［雄鶏］	ondori
duck	アヒル	ahiru
drake	雄アヒル	oahiru
goose	ガチョウ	gachō
tom turkey	雄七面鳥	oshichimenchō
turkey (hen)	七面鳥［シチメンチョウ］	shichimenchō
domestic animals	家畜	kachiku
tame (e.g., ~ hamster)	馴れた	nare ta
to tame (vt)	かいならす	kainarasu
to breed (vt)	飼養する	shiyō suru
farm	農場	nōjō
poultry	家禽	kakin
cattle	畜牛	chiku gyū
herd (cattle)	群れ	mure
stable	馬小屋	umagoya
pigsty	豚小屋	buta goya
cowshed	牛舎	gyūsha
rabbit hutch	ウサギ小屋	usagi koya
hen house	鶏小屋	niwatori goya

90. Birds

bird	鳥	tori
pigeon	鳩 [ハト]	hato
sparrow	スズメ (雀)	suzume
tit	シジュウカラ [四十雀]	shijūkara
magpie	カササギ (鵲)	kasasagi
raven	ワタリガラス [渡鴉]	watari garasu
crow	カラス [鴉]	karasu
jackdaw	ニシコクマルガラス	nishikokumaru garasu
rook	ミヤマガラス [深山烏]	miyama garasu
duck	カモ [鴨]	kamo
goose	ガチョウ	gachō
pheasant	キジ	kiji
eagle	鷲	washi
hawk	鷹	taka
falcon	ハヤブサ [隼]	hayabusa
vulture	ハゲワシ	hagewashi
condor (Andean ~)	コンドル	kondoru
swan	白鳥 [ハクチョウ]	hakuchō
crane	鶴 [ツル]	tsuru
stork	シュバシコウ	shubashikō
parrot	オウム	ōmu
hummingbird	ハチドリ [蜂鳥]	hachidori
peacock	クジャク [孔雀]	kujaku
ostrich	ダチョウ [駝鳥]	dachō
heron	サギ [鷺]	sagi
flamingo	フラミンゴ	furamingo
pelican	ペリカン	perikan
nightingale	サヨナキドリ	sayonakidori
swallow	ツバメ [燕]	tsubame
thrush	ノハラツグミ	nohara tsugumi
song thrush	ウタツグミ [歌鶫]	uta tsugumi
blackbird	クロウタドリ	kurōtadori
swift	アマツバメ [雨燕]	ama tsubame
lark	ヒバリ [雲雀]	hibari
quail	ウズラ	uzura
woodpecker	キツツキ	kitsutsuki
cuckoo	カッコウ [郭公]	kakkō
owl	トラフズク	torafuzuku
eagle owl	ワシミミズク	washi mimizuku

wood grouse	ヨーロッパ オオライチョウ	yōroppa ōraichō
black grouse	クロライチョウ	kuro raichō
partridge	ヨーロッパヤマウズラ	yōroppa yamauzura
starling	ムクドリ	mukudori
canary	カナリア [金糸雀]	kanaria
hazel grouse	エゾライチョウ	ezo raichō
chaffinch	ズアオアトリ	zuaoatori
bullfinch	ウソ [鷽]	uso
seagull	カモメ [鷗]	kamome
albatross	アホウドリ	ahōdori
penguin	ペンギン	pengin

91. Fish. Marine animals

bream	ブリーム	burīmu
carp	コイ [鯉]	koi
perch	ヨーロピアンパーチ	yōropian pāchi
catfish	ナマズ	namazu
pike	カワカマス	kawakamasu
salmon	サケ	sake
sturgeon	チョウザメ [蝶鮫]	chōzame
herring	ニシン	nishin
Atlantic salmon	タイセイヨウサケ [大西洋鮭]	taiseiyō sake
mackerel	サバ [鯖]	saba
flatfish	カレイ [鰈]	karei
zander, pike perch	ザンダー	zandā
cod	タラ [鱈]	tara
tuna	マグロ [鮪]	maguro
trout	マス [鱒]	masu
eel	ウナギ [鰻]	unagi
electric ray	シビレエイ	shibireei
moray eel	ウツボ [鱓]	utsubo
piranha	ピラニア	pirania
shark	サメ [鮫]	same
dolphin	イルカ [海豚]	iruka
whale	クジラ [鯨]	kujira
crab	カニ [蟹]	kani
jellyfish	クラゲ [水母]	kurage
octopus	タコ [蛸]	tako
starfish	ヒトデ [海星]	hitode

| sea urchin | ウニ［海胆］ | uni |
| seahorse | タツノオトシゴ | tatsunootoshigo |

oyster	カキ［牡蠣］	kaki
shrimp	エビ	ebi
lobster	イセエビ	iseebi
spiny lobster	スパイニーロブスター	supainī robusutā

92. Amphibians. Reptiles

| snake | ヘビ（蛇） | hebi |
| venomous (snake) | 毒…、 有毒な | doku…, yūdoku na |

viper	クサリヘビ	kusarihebi
cobra	コブラ	kobura
python	ニシキヘビ	nishikihebi
boa	ボア	boa

grass snake	ヨーロッパヤマカガシ	yōroppa yamakagashi
rattle snake	ガラガラヘビ	garagarahebi
anaconda	アナコンダ	anakonda

lizard	トカゲ［蜥蜴］	tokage
iguana	イグアナ	iguana
monitor lizard	オオトカゲ	ōtokage
salamander	サンショウウオ［山椒魚］	sanshōuo
chameleon	カメレオン	kamereon
scorpion	サソリ［蠍］	sasori

turtle	カメ［亀］	kame
frog	蛙［カエル］	kaeru
toad	ヒキガエル	hikigaeru
crocodile	ワニ［鰐］	wani

93. Insects

insect, bug	昆虫	konchū
butterfly	チョウ［蝶］	chō
ant	アリ［蟻］	ari
fly	ハエ［蝿］	hae
mosquito	カ［蚊］	ka
beetle	甲虫	kabutomushi

wasp	ワスプ	wasupu
bee	ハチ［蜂］	hachi
bumblebee	マルハナバチ［丸花蜂］	maruhanabachi
gadfly	アブ［虻］	abu
spider	クモ［蜘蛛］	kumo

spider's web	クモの巣	kumo no su
dragonfly	トンボ [蜻蛉]	tonbo
grasshopper	キリギリス	kirigirisu
moth (night butterfly)	ガ [蛾]	ga
cockroach	ゴキブリ [蜚蠊]	gokiburi
tick	ダニ [壁蝨、蜱]	dani
flea	ノミ [蚤]	nomi
midge	ヌカカ [糠蚊]	nukaka
locust	バッタ [飛蝗]	batta
snail	カタツムリ [蝸牛]	katatsumuri
cricket	コオロギ [蟋蟀、蛬]	kōrogi
lightning bug	ホタル [蛍、螢]	hotaru
ladybug	テントウムシ [天道虫]	tentōmushi
cockchafer	コフキコガネ	kofukikogane
leech	ヒル [蛭]	hiru
caterpillar	ケムシ [毛虫]	kemushi
earthworm	ミミズ [蚯蚓]	mimizu
larva	幼虫	yōchū

FLORA

94. Trees

tree	木	ki
deciduous (adj)	落葉性の	rakuyō sei no
coniferous (adj)	針葉樹の	shinyōju no
evergreen (adj)	常緑の	jōryoku no
apple tree	りんごの木	ringonoki
pear tree	洋梨の木	yōnashinoki
sweet cherry tree	セイヨウミザクラ	seiyōmi zakura
sour cherry tree	スミミザクラ	sumimi zakura
plum tree	プラムトリー	puramu torī
birch	カバノキ	kabanoki
oak	オーク	ōku
linden tree	シナノキ [科の木]	shinanoki
aspen	ヤマナラシ [山鳴らし]	yamanarashi
maple	カエデ [楓]	kaede
spruce	スプルース	supurūsu
pine	マツ [松]	matsu
larch	カラマツ [唐松]	karamatsu
fir tree	モミ [樅]	momi
cedar	シダー	shidā
poplar	ポプラ	popura
rowan	ナナカマド	nanakamado
willow	ヤナギ [柳]	yanagi
alder	ハンノキ	hannoki
beech	ブナ	buna
elm	ニレ [楡]	nire
ash (tree)	トネリコ [梣]	toneriko
chestnut	クリ [栗]	kuri
magnolia	モクレン [木蓮]	mokuren
palm tree	ヤシ [椰子]	yashi
cypress	イトスギ [糸杉]	itosugi
mangrove	マングローブ	mangurōbu
baobab	バオバブ	baobabu
eucalyptus	ユーカリ	yūkari
sequoia	セコイア	sekoia

95. Shrubs

bush	低木	teiboku
shrub	潅木	kanboku
grapevine	ブドウ ［葡萄］	budō
vineyard	ブドウ園 ［葡萄園］	budōen
raspberry bush	ラズベリー	razuberī
blackcurrant bush	クロスグリ	kuro suguri
redcurrant bush	フサスグリ	fusa suguri
gooseberry bush	セイヨウスグリ	seiyō suguri
acacia	アカシア	akashia
barberry	メギ	megi
jasmine	ジャスミン	jasumin
juniper	セイヨウネズ	seiyōnezu
rosebush	バラの木	baranoki
dog rose	イヌバラ	inu bara

96. Fruits. Berries

fruit	果物	kudamono
fruits	果物	kudamono
apple	リンゴ	ringo
pear	洋梨	yōnashi
plum	プラム	puramu
strawberry	イチゴ（苺）	ichigo
cherry	チェリー	cherī
sour cherry	サワー チェリー	sawā cherī
sweet cherry	スイート チェリー	suīto cherī
grape	ブドウ［葡萄］	budō
raspberry	ラズベリー（木苺）	razuberī
blackcurrant	クロスグリ	kuro suguri
redcurrant	フサスグリ	fusa suguri
gooseberry	セイヨウスグリ	seiyō suguri
cranberry	クランベリー	kuranberī
orange	オレンジ	orenji
mandarin	マンダリン	mandarin
pineapple	パイナップル	painappuru
banana	バナナ	banana
date	デーツ	dētsu
lemon	レモン	remon
apricot	アンズ［杏子］	anzu

peach	モモ［桃］	momo
kiwi	キウイ	kiui
grapefruit	グレープフルーツ	gurēbu furūtsu
berry	ベリー	berī
berries	ベリー	berī
cowberry	コケモモ	kokemomo
field strawberry	ノイチゴ［野いちご］	noichigo
bilberry	ビルベリー	biruberī

97. Flowers. Plants

flower	花	hana
bouquet (of flowers)	花束	hanataba
rose (flower)	バラ	bara
tulip	チューリップ	chūrippu
carnation	カーネーション	kānēshon
gladiolus	グラジオラス	gurajiorasu
cornflower	ヤグルマギク［矢車菊］	yagurumagiku
bluebell	ホタルブクロ	hotarubukuro
dandelion	タンポポ［蒲公英］	tanpopo
camomile	カモミール	kamomīru
aloe	アロエ	aroe
cactus	サボテン	saboten
rubber plant, ficus	イチジク	ichijiku
lily	ユリ［百合］	yuri
geranium	ゼラニウム	zeranyūmu
hyacinth	ヒヤシンス	hiyashinsu
mimosa	ミモザ	mimoza
narcissus	スイセン［水仙］	suisen
nasturtium	キンレンカ［金蓮花］	kinrenka
orchid	ラン［蘭］	ran
peony	シャクヤク［芍薬］	shakuyaku
violet	スミレ［菫］	sumire
pansy	パンジー	panjī
forget-me-not	ワスレナグサ［勿忘草］	wasurenagusa
daisy	デイジー	deijī
poppy	ポピー	popī
hemp	アサ［麻］	asa
mint	ミント	minto
lily of the valley	スズラン［鈴蘭］	suzuran
snowdrop	スノードロップ	sunōdoroppu

nettle	イラクサ［刺草］	irakusa
sorrel	スイバ	suiba
water lily	スイレン［睡蓮］	suiren
fern	シダ	shida
lichen	地衣類	chī rui
tropical greenhouse	温室	onshitsu
grass lawn	芝生	shibafu
flowerbed	花壇	kadan
plant	植物	shokubutsu
grass, herb	草	kusa
blade of grass	草の葉	kusa no ha
leaf	葉	ha
petal	花びら	hanabira
stem	茎	kuki
tuber	塊茎	kaikei
young plant (shoot)	シュート	shūto
thorn	茎針	kuki hari
to blossom (vi)	開花する	kaika suru
to fade, to wither	しおれる	shioreru
smell (odor)	香り	kaori
to cut (flowers)	切る	kiru
to pick (a flower)	摘む	tsumamu

98. Cereals, grains

grain	穀物	kokumotsu
cereal crops	禾穀類	kakokurui
ear (of barley, etc.)	花穂	kasui
wheat	コムギ［小麦］	komugi
rye	ライムギ［ライ麦］	raimugi
oats	オーツムギ［オーツ麦］	ōtsu mugi
millet	キビ［黍］	kibi
barley	オオムギ［大麦］	ōmugi
corn	トウモロコシ	tōmorokoshi
rice	イネ［稲］	ine
buckwheat	ソバ［蕎麦］	soba
pea plant	エンドウ［豌豆］	endō
kidney bean	インゲンマメ［隠元豆］	ingen mame
soy	ダイズ［大豆］	daizu
lentil	レンズマメ［レンズ豆］	renzu mame
beans (pulse crops)	豆類	mamerui

COUNTRIES OF THE WORLD

99. Countries. Part 1

Afghanistan	アフガニスタン	afuganisutan
Albania	アルバニア	arubania
Argentina	アルゼンチン	aruzenchin
Armenia	アルメニア	arumenia
Australia	オーストラリア	ōsutoraria
Austria	オーストリア	ōsutoria
Azerbaijan	アゼルバイジャン	azerubaijan
The Bahamas	バハマ	bahama
Bangladesh	バングラデシュ	banguradeshu
Belarus	ベラルーシー	berarūshī
Belgium	ベルギー	berugī
Bolivia	ボリビア	boribia
Bosnia-Herzegovina	ボスニア・ヘルツェゴヴィナ	bosunia herutsegovina
Brazil	ブラジル	burajiru
Bulgaria	ブルガリア	burugaria
Cambodia	カンボジア	kanbojia
Canada	カナダ	kanada
Chile	チリ	chiri
China	中国	chūgoku
Colombia	コロンビア	koronbia
Croatia	クロアチア	kuroachia
Cuba	キューバ	kyūba
Cyprus	キプロス	kipurosu
Czech Republic	チェコ	cheko
Denmark	デンマーク	denmāku
Dominican Republic	ドミニカ共和国	dominikakyōwakoku
Ecuador	エクアドル	ekuadoru
Egypt	エジプト	ejiputo
England	イギリス	igirisu
Estonia	エストニア	esutonia
Finland	フィンランド	finrando
France	フランス	furansu
French Polynesia	フランス領ポリネシア	furansu ryō porineshia
Georgia	グルジア	gurujia
Germany	ドイツ	doitsu
Ghana	ガーナ	gāna
Great Britain	グレートブリテン島	gurētoburiten tō

Greece	ギリシャ	girisha
Haiti	ハイチ	haichi
Hungary	ハンガリー	hangarī

100. Countries. Part 2

Iceland	アイスランド	aisurando
India	インド	indo
Indonesia	インドネシア	indoneshia
Iran	イラン	iran
Iraq	イラク	iraku
Ireland	アイルランド	airurando
Israel	イスラエル	isuraeru
Italy	イタリア	itaria

Jamaica	ジャマイカ	jamaika
Japan	日本	nihon
Jordan	ヨルダン	yorudan
Kazakhstan	カザフスタン	kazafusutan
Kenya	ケニア	kenia
Kirghizia	キルギス	kirugisu
Kuwait	クウェート	kuwēto

Laos	ラオス	raosu
Latvia	ラトビア	ratobia
Lebanon	レバノン	rebanon
Libya	リビア	ribia
Liechtenstein	リヒテンシュタイン	rihitenshutain
Lithuania	リトアニア	ritoania
Luxembourg	ルクセンブルク	rukusenburuku

Macedonia	マケドニア地方	makedonia chihō
Madagascar	マダガスカル	madagasukaru
Malaysia	マレーシア	marēshia
Malta	マルタ	maruta
Mexico	メキシコ	mekishiko
Moldavia	モルドヴァ	morudova

Monaco	モナコ	monako
Mongolia	モンゴル	mongoru
Montenegro	モンテネグロ	monteneguro
Morocco	モロッコ	morokko
Myanmar	ミャンマー	myanmā

Namibia	ナミビア	namibia
Nepal	ネパール	nepāru
Netherlands	ネーデルラント	nēderuranto
New Zealand	ニュージーランド	nyūjīrando
North Korea	北朝鮮	kitachōsen
Norway	ノルウェー	noruwē

101. Countries. Part 3

Pakistan	パキスタン	pakisutan
Palestine	パレスチナ	paresuchina
Panama	パナマ	panama
Paraguay	パラグアイ	paraguai
Peru	ペルー	perū
Poland	ポーランド	pōrando
Portugal	ポルトガル	porutogaru
Romania	ルーマニア	rūmania
Russia	ロシア	roshia
Saudi Arabia	サウジアラビア	saujiarabia
Scotland	スコットランド	sukottorando
Senegal	セネガル	senegaru
Serbia	セルビア	serubia
Slovakia	スロバキア	surobakia
Slovenia	スロベニア	surobenia
South Africa	南アフリカ	minami afurika
South Korea	大韓民国	daikanminkoku
Spain	スペイン	supein
Suriname	スリナム	surinamu
Sweden	スウェーデン	suwēden
Switzerland	スイス	suisu
Syria	シリア	shiria
Taiwan	台湾	taiwan
Tajikistan	タジキスタン	tajikisutan
Tanzania	タンザニア	tanzania
Tasmania	タスマニア	tasumania
Thailand	タイ	tai
Tunisia	チュニジア	chunijia
Turkey	トルコ	toruko
Turkmenistan	トルクメニスタン	torukumenisutan
Ukraine	ウクライナ	ukuraina
United Arab Emirates	アラブ首長国連邦	arabu shuchō koku renpō
United States of America	アメリカ合衆国	amerika gasshūkoku
Uruguay	ウルグアイ	uruguai
Uzbekistan	ウズベキスタン	uzubekisutan
Vatican	バチカン	bachikan
Venezuela	ベネズエラ	benezuera
Vietnam	ベトナム	betonamu
Zanzibar	ザンジバル	zanjibaru

CPSIA information can be obtained
at www.ICGtesting.com
Printed in the USA
LVOW01s0227260716
497794LV00034B/876/P